Danger—Girls Working!

A MYSTERY COMEDY FOR WOMEN

By James Reach

SAMUEL FRENCH, INC.

45 WEST 25TH STREET   NEW YORK 10010
7623 SUNSET BOULEVARD HOLLYWOOD 90046
LONDON   TORONTO

DANGER—GIRLS WORKING!

STORY OF THE PLAY

A new play with a highly novel idea which is sure to appeal to any group of girls or women. Although two of the characters are middle-aged, the play can easily be done by clubs of high-school age. The setting and properties are extremely simple. The scene is "Mrs. McCarthy's Boarding House for Girls" in New York, permitting the introduction of many varied and interesting types, all striving to make their way in the big city. There is the newspaper woman who wants to write a novel. There is the wise-cracking shop girl. There is the waitress with aching feet. There are the serious music student, the faded actress, the girl looking for romance, the kid from the South who wants to crash Broadway, and others. Mrs. McCarthy, the landlady, is also the proud custodian of the "McCarthy Collection," a group of perfect uncut diamonds. When the "McCarthy Collection" disappears from the safe, the newspaper woman is given two hours to solve the case before the police are called. Suspicion is cleverly shifted from one to the other of the girls; then, just before the second hour—and the third act—is over, a very surprising solution is arrived at. The play has suspense, quickness of pace, many good laughs—everything a mystery should have. And the dialogue and characterizations are exceptionally good.

CHARACTERS
(In Order of Appearance)

ARLENE DAY, *a sales girl.*
SELENA BARNES, *a waitress.*
GRAYCE JOHNSTON, *a music student.*
ROSIE, *a maid.*
HANNAH WILLIAMS, *a romantic young lady.*
PHYLLIS DEERING, *a newspaper woman.*
CLAUDIA VANDERMEER, *a home girl.*
MRS. MCCARTHY, *a landlady.*
LULU ANN SMITH, *a girl from the South.*
MISS VERNE, *a woman of mystery.*
RAY CARTWRIGHT, *an actress.*

SYNOPSIS OF ACTS

The action of the entire play takes place in the lounging room of Mrs. McCarthy's Boarding House for Girls.

ACT I. *Early evening on a Spring day in the present year.*
ACT II. *Several days later. Sunday. Late in the morning.*
ACT III. *Immediately following Act II. No elapsed time.*

DESCRIPTION OF CHARACTERS

ARLENE *is a girl of twenty-one. Very quick on the trigger. Has a shrewd sense of humor with a dry, humorous way of speaking. In dress and appearance a typical shop girl.*

SELENA *is a girl of twenty-one. Probably small and plump in appearance, not unattractive and speaks in a high, squeaky voice with a lisp. Should be a good foil for Arlene.*

GRAYCE *is a girl in her early twenties. Tall and thin, severe in speech and appearance, and wears conservative clothes. Horn-rimmed spectacles and a plain hair-comb.*

ROSIE *is a woman either young or middle-aged. Teutonic type, stout, tidy in appearance, her cheeks usually flushed, very slow-witted.*

HANNAH *is an attractive girl of twenty. Tall and willowy, and wears attractive clothes. Her manner should be exuberant and breathless. She never walks, but flutters; never talks, but gushes.*

PHYLLIS *is a girl of twenty-three. Has a nice appearance, rather quiet charm, good sense of humor and intelligent manner.*

CLAUDIA *is a girl of twenty-two. Tall, blonde, nicely-built and attractive in a rather obvious way. Slinky and langorous in her manner, and always posing.*

MRS. McCARTHY *is a woman of forty-five. Stout and buxom, but the live-wire type. Not overly intelligent, with a penchant for talking a great deal.*

7

LULU ANN *is a girl of eighteen. Small, dark, wispy and very charming. Has a winsome smile, a ready laugh and speaks with a pleasing southern accent.*

MISS VERNE *is a girl of about twenty-five. Wears conservative business clothes, and is a little mannish in appearance. Her manner is secretive and she gives the impression of being well able to take care of herself.*

RAY *is a woman of about forty. Was probably a beauty in her day, but now her charm is rather faded, her clothes shabby. In voice and manner, she is a cultivated, intelligent person.*

DANGER—GIRLS WORKING!

ACT ONE

THE TIME: *A Spring day in the present year. Early evening.*

THE PLACE: *The lounge in "Mrs. McCarthy's Boarding House for Girls." A room furnished in typical rooming-house style, with furniture overstuffed and a little shabby. The one entrance to the room is a large double door, or arch, midway of the back wall; this leads on the Right to the bedrooms, and on the Left to the downstairs rooms of the house. A row of windows in the Left wall. Grand piano and bench in the corner up Right. Up Left a small table; on the table a reading lamp; either side of the table an armchair. Stage Center a long library table which is littered with magazines, newspapers, etc. In the corner down Right a divan and behind it a floor lamp. Down Left another armchair. Outside the arch, and in view of the audience, a small console table on which is a telephone.*

AT RISE: GRAYCE, ARLENE *and* SELENA *are discovered.* GRAYCE *is at the piano, playing softly a waltz by Chopin.* ARLENE *is seated in the divan, an open newspaper in her lap.* SELENA *is seated in the chair down* R., *with one of her shoes off.*

9

ARLENE. So I give her one of my best smiles and I says to her, "Madam, this is the very finest pure silk gown we have at a dollar-ninety-five." So then she freezes up and says, "I'm going straight to the manager—"

SELENA. *(Rubbing her foot)* Oh, my poor feet—they hurt tho bad.

ARLENE. Honest, Hon, I was fit to be tied. Can you imagine? I show her every dress in the department, and then she pulls a crack like that.

SELENA. Well, I don't thee what you're complaining about—

ARLENE. Complaining? After what I've been through? I only wish I could have told that old battle-axe just what I thought of her.

SELENA. After waiting on tableth all day at Wilde's, your bargain bathement would theem like heaven to me, Arlene.

ARLENE. Yeah? Well, that's where we differ, Hon.

SELENA. That new thirty-five thent table de hote lunch hath brought in every thenographer in the neighborhood, and you know that crowd—not a tip in a carload.

GRAYCE. *(Frigidly)* Is it possible to have a little quiet in here—just a little?

ARLENE. Oops! There goes Mrs. Pader-roos-ski. Gosh, Grayce, I should think you'd know that piece backwards by this time.

GRAYCE. Well, I've got to practice. I—I've got to practice.

ARLENE. Why?

GRAYCE. Why? *Why?* Don't be silly, Arlene. You know one can't get anywhere at all in music without practice. Why, look at all the great artists. Look at Rachmaninoff. Look at—

ARLENE. All right. I'm convinced.

SELENA. What'th the name of that pieth, Grayth?

GRAYCE. Waltz—by Chopin.

SELENA. Oh, ith that by Chopin? Why didn't you tell me? I love hith muthic, don't you, Arlene?

ARLENE. Personally, to me it don't mean a thing if it ain't got that swing.

GRAYCE. I wish you'd let me concentrate, Arlene. Heaven knows I get little enough time to practice as it is.

ARLENE. All right. Go ahead and concentrate. *(Looks through her newspaper.)*

GRAYCE. Thanks. *(She plays; the OTHERS are silent for a moment.)*

ARLENE. You know, you wouldn't be so bad at the piano, Hon, if you'd learn to jazz it up a little. Why don't you try a nice hot number by Irving Berlin, or someone like that?

GRAYCE. *(Bangs a discord)* Really, Arlene—! *(Rises)* Irving Berlin! *(Angrily crosses to table up L. and sits down.)*

ARLENE. What's the matter now? I thought you needed the practice so bad.

GRAYCE. I'll wait. (ARLENE *shrugs; leafs through her newspaper.)*

SELENA. Oh, don't mind her, Grayth. She doethn't apprethiate good muthic when she hearth it.

GRAYCE. Yes. I quite realize that, Selena.

SELENA. When are you giving that conthert at Town Hall?

GRAYCE. I don't know. Just as soon as I can raise five hundred dollars.

SELENA. Raise it? You mean you have to pay for your own conthert?

GRAYCE. Yes. Oh, the whole thing is so unfair, Selena. Talent, genius—they mean nothing if you haven't got five hundred dollars. What's the use of being a great musician if nobody ever knows about it?

SELENA. You muthn't talk like that, Grayth. Why, thome day—

GRAYCE. Yes, some day. And in the meantime, I can just shrivel up and rot for all anybody cares.

SELENA. You know what they thay: "If at firtht you don't thuctheed—"

GRACE. *(Sighs)* Oh, I suppose I'll go on trying. I suppose I'll go on working in a horrible, stuffy office at eighteen dollars per, going without decent clothes, without lunches, so I can save enough to give my concert. But, when I do—well, you just watch them sit up and take notice.

SELENA. That'th the way to talk. Be an optomitht, like me. *(Draws her breath in pain)* Oh, my poor feet! *(Rubs her foot)* M'mm! That feelth good!

ARLENE. *(Reading from paper)* "Fillet mignon, sauce de espagnol, lyonaise potatoes with cream sauce—"

SELENA. What'th that, Arlene?

ARLENE. Oh, I'm just reading tonight's menu at the Ritz Hotel, Hon. *(Reads)* "Whole broiled baby lobster, roast stuffed capon—"

SELENA. Thtop, you're breaking my heart!

ARLENE. "Roast stuffed capon"—people really do eat food like that, don't they?

SELENA. Wait until your Printh Charming cometh along, Arlene.

ARLENE. Prince Charming—in Himmelberger's Bargain Basement? I'm afraid I'll have a long wait, Hon.

SELENA. Me, too. Did you ever thee the kind of men that eat thirty-five thent table de hotes?

ARLENE. You're too particular. I'm here to tell you any kind of men look good after you've been fighting off armies of crazy bargain hunters.

GRAYCE. I wonder what's on *our* menu tonight. *(Sighs)* Hash again, I suppose.

SELENA. I don't think tho. We've had it three

nighth in a row now. Even Mithith McCarthy can't make hash latht forever.

ARLENE. Maybe not, but she can make a darned good effort.

(ROSIE enters c. from R. Has a tablecloth over her arm.)

SELENA. There'th Rosie. Let'th athk her. Rosie!

ROSIE. *(Coming into arch)* Yah? You vant something?

ARLENE. We just wanted to know what the old gal's got cooked up for tonight, Hon.

ROSIE. *(Puzzled)* "Old gel—" *(Beams)* Oh, you mean Mrs. McCarthy, ain't it?

ARLENE. You catch on quick.

SELENA. And don't you dare tell uth we're having hash again.

ROSIE. Oh, no—no hash. Tonight it gives a big surprise—

ARLENE. Surprise?

ROSIE. Ach, yes. Something much better than hash —meat loaf!

GRAYCE. That's a welcome change, isn't it?

HANNAH. *(Enters c. from L. in street clothes)* Hello, kids!

OTHERS. Hello, Hannah!

HANNAH. Dinner ready yet, Rosie?

ROSIE. Not yet, but soon. I call you. Excuse me, I must set the table vonce. *(Exits c. to L.)*

HANNAH. Say, kids, you'll never guess what happened to me today.

ARLENE. A man.

HANNAH. *(Surprised)* Why, yes. How did you know, Arlene?

ARLENE. You've got that gleam in your eyes, Hon. It never fails.

HANNAH. Well, but really, this was the most *marvelous* man.

ARLENE. Yeah, they always are.

HANNAH. You should have seen him, kids: tall, slender, dark blue eyes, wavy black hair, and the most adorable little mole right under his chin—

ARLENE. You certainly got a close look, didn't you, Hon?

HANNAH. Everything about him is simply fascinating—even his name. Sylvester Crookingham—

ARLENE. What's that?

HANNAH. Why, that's his name, Arlene—Sylvester Crookingham.

ARLENE. I thought that's what you said, but it didn't seem possible.

HANNAH. Really, the whole thing was so *romantic,* kids—just like one of those magazine stories, or something. And to think it should have happened to me.

SELENA. How did you meet him, Hannah?

HANNAH. *(Vaguely)* Meet him? Oh, he just sort of walked into the office, I guess.

ARLENE. Sure, it's easy, Hon, if you know how.

HANNAH. He walked into the office, and he looked at me with those marvelous, soulful eyes of his and he said to me, "Little lady—I think I've got ulcers of the stomach."

ARLENE. That certainly was romantic, all right.

HANNAH. Wasn't it? Well, I made an appointment for him to see Doctor Farley, and then we just sat around and talked for a while—about his ulcers.

ARLENE. Yeah, you meet a nice class of people, working in a doctor's office.

HANNAH. Oh, you do. I wouldn't trade my job for any other in the world. The most romantic things are always happening to me. It's wonderful.

PHYLLIS. *(Enters* C. *from* R. *She is carrying three books)* Hello, there!

OTHERS. Hello, Phyllis. Good evening, Phil. *(Etc.)*

PHYLLIS. Am I early for dinner?

SELENA. Yeth. Rosie's jutht thetting the table. We're having meat loaf.

PHYLLIS. Well, that should be just lovely. *(Sits at table up L. with GRAYCE.)*

HANNAH. Dinner—? Oh, I've got to fly, kids. Sylvester is calling for me at eight.

SELENA. You jutht met him today, and you've got a date with him tonight?

HANNAH. Certainly. Oh, he's a perfect gentleman—I wouldn't go out with him if he weren't. He's got two tickets to the Veterinarians' Convention.

ARLENE. Veterinarian? You mean the boy friend's a horse doctor?

HANNAH. Yes, didn't I tell you? He's a big veterinarian from upstate somewhere. But, honestly, he's the most distinguished-looking man. I was just telling the kids about the most romantic thing that happened to me, Phil—

PHYLLIS. Again?

ARLENE. Yeah, and it all began with stomach ulcers.

HANNAH. Honestly, things always seem to happen to me—I don't know why. Oh, Phil, would you mind awfully if I borrowed your blue formal? Mine's at the cleaners, and I simply have to look my best for Sylvester, and—

PHYLLIS. Help yourself, Hannah. You know where it is.

HANNAH. Thanks loads. I've got to fly— *(Crosses up to arch)* Oh, dear, I just remembered—I haven't one single pair of stockings without a run— Now what will I do without stockings—?

GRAYCE. There's an extra pair in the second drawer of my dresser.

HANNAH. *(Fluttering about)* Oh, thanks, Grayce dear—that's so nice of you. Well, I've got to fly— My, I'm so excited! I'll see you all at dinner— Excuse me— *(Exits c. to r.)*

SELENA. She thertainly hath a marvelouth time, doethn't she?

ARLENE. Yeah, she can find romance in the most unusual places.

PHYLLIS. It's nice being like Hannah. She was born wearing a pair of rose-colored glasses, and she's been wearing them ever since.

ARLENE. Some day somebody's going to tell her there isn't any Santa Claus, and she'll just die of a broken heart.

PHYLLIS. But think of all the fun she'll have first.

GRAYCE. *(Looks curiously at* PHYLLIS' *books)* What are you reading, Phyllis?

PHYLLIS. Nothing that would interest you, Grayce. *(Reads off the titles)* The Case of the Archbishop's Antelope. About the Murder of a Cross-eyed Comedian. And this one is Death at the Dime Museum.

GRAYCE. Heavens! Murder mysteries?

PHYLLIS. Just doing a little research. I like to take them apart and see what makes them click. Like practically everybody else, I intend to write a book myself some day.

ARLENE. How's everything on the newspaper?

PHYLLIS. Just about as dull as ever, darling.

SELENA. Are you thtill writing that column of houth-hold hinth? What'th the name of it again—?

PHYLLIS. *Grandma's Favorite Recipes.* Yes, I'm still writing it, Selena. But one of these days I'll have every cook-book in print exhausted of its recipes, and then I'll be looking for a job.

SELENA. Well, whatever you do, thtay away from thirty-five thent rethtauranth.

ARLENE. And bargain basements.

PHYLLIS. Yes, I suppose it's just another case of that old saw about "The grass being greener—" and so forth.

GRAYCE. But, Phyllis, don't tell me a person of your intelligence is going to write one of those awful murder mysteries.

PHYLLIS. Sure. Why not?

GRAYCE. I should think you might try to do something a little more worth while.

PHYLLIS. And starve to death? No, thanks. Everyone reads mysteries—that's where the money is.

SELENA. I think mysteries are thwell, ethpecially when there'th oodleth of blood and loth of dead bodieth.

PHYLLIS. There, you see, Grayce? The great reading public speaks.

GRAYCE. Well, if you want to prostitute your art before the almighty dollar sign, then I suppose it's no concern of mine. *(Rises and crosses to the piano.)*

PHYLLIS. Ouch!

ARLENE. Why don't you write a book about this place, Hon? You could call it, *The Case of Mrs. McCarthy's Boarding House for Girls.*

PHYLLIS. That's an idea.

SELENA. You'd thertainly have plenty of odd characterth.

PHYLLIS. But no plot. Nothing ever happens here.

ARLENE. Maybe we could arrange a nice little murder for you. I can think of one or two likely victims without half trying. (GRAYCE *bangs a discord on the piano.)*

PHYLLIS. I'm afraid Grayce doesn't find our conversation very elevating, girls.

GRAYCE. I most certainly do not. (ROSIE *crosses past arch from* L. *She has some linen over her arm.)*

ARLENE. Hey, Rosie, are you trying to starve us out?

Rosie. Soon, soon it be ready. I got to fix up a room. Ve joost got a new roomer.

Selena. A new roomer? Who ith it?

Rosie. Oh, joost some girl.

Arlene. Well, thanks, Hon. That tells us everything we want to know.

Rosie. Yah, yah, excuse me. I got lots to do vonce. *(TELEPHONE rings.)* Oh, der telephone. *(*All *but* Grayce *rise and start for it.)* I answer it. *(Crosses to it.)*

Arlene. If that's a man, don't let him get away.

Rosie. Yah, yah, don't vorry. *(Picks up receiver.)* Hollo— Yah?—This is Mrs. McCarthy's boarding house—for girls— Vhat's dot?—She's downstairs. Ve joost got a new roomer und— Vhat?—Oh, you vant to speak to Miss Johnston—

Selena. It'th for you, Grayth. *(The* Others *take their seats again.)*

Rosie. Yah, yah, she's here. Joost von minutes, please. *(Puts down receiver and comes into room.)*

Grayce. Thank you. *(Crosses to telephone.)*

Rosie. Yah, I go now. I got to fix up der room. It's der last room ve got, und it's going to be a job. *(Exits* c. *to* r.*)*

Grayce. *(In telephone)* Hello— Who?—Oh, yes, the concert— *(Looks out into room, trying to keep the others from hearing)* Well—er—I'm not sure— Yes, I *said* I'd have it, but— Well, I'll try— Perhaps— No, not tomorrow— I'll have to let you know. I—I can't talk very well now— Yes, I will. Goodbye. *(Hangs up and comes into arch.)*

Selena. Oh, wath it about the conthert?

Grayce. *(Curtly)* It was—nothing. Pardon me— I want to get ready for dinner, if you don't mind. *(Exits* c. *to* r.*)*

Arlene. Well, what's eating her? Why all the secrecy?

Selena. Oh, it'th jutht one of her moods.

PHYLLIS. Poor Grayce and her concert. If she ever does give it, and it's a flop—I'm afraid that would be the end of her.

SELENA. She thertainly hath got her heart thet on it.

ARLENE. *(Rises and crosses up to arch)* And I've got my heart set on food, food! Ye gods! The service we get around here—

PHYLLIS. Well, darling, you can hardly expect lobster and personal maids at the money.

ARLENE. I don't, Hon, but— *(Looking off R.)* Oops! Here comes the duchess. *(Comes swaggering down; in mocking voice)* Oh, my dear, I'm so bored with it all, doncha know— (CLAUDIA *enters* C. *from* R.) Hello, Hon! We were just talking about you.

CLAUDIA. *(Wearing house coat and slippers)* Oh, really? *(Sinks wearily down in divan.)*

ARLENE. Isn't it a little early for you to be up?

CLAUDIA. Oh, dear, no! I've been about for hours.

ARLENE. Fancy that.

CLAUDIA. Yes, I woke up at—noon, I think it was —and I couldn't for the life of me fall asleep again.

ARLENE. T'st, t'st! Practically the break of dawn.

CLAUDIA. So I got up and answered a few want ads.

PHYLLIS. Not actually thinking of going to work, Claudia?

CLAUDIA. Yes, just for the fun of it, you know. Not that I actually need a job of course—

PHYLLIS. Oh, of course not.

CLAUDIA. But things get so boring, doncha know, when one has the whole day to oneself.

ARLENE. Yeah, ain't it awful, Hon?

CLAUDIA. *(Smothers a deep yawn)* Oh, dear! Those crowds downtown are so exhausting. I don't see how you girls ever put up with it.

ARLENE. I often wonder about that.

CLAUDIA. Oh, Selena, be a good girl and hand me

one of those magazines from the table, won't you? (SELENA *gives her an indignant look, but gets a magazine from table* C. *and gives it to her.* CLAUDIA *looks at it)* Oh, dear no—I've seen this. One of those others, please. Isn't it drafty in here? Arlene, be a good girl and shut that window—

MRS. McCARTHY. *(Enters* C. *from* L. *with* LULU ANN. *The latter is carrying a suitcase.)* This is our lounge, dearie. You'll always find something doing in here. Now, you just set your bag down right there and come in and meet the girls.

LULU ANN. All rightie. *(Puts her bag down outside of the arch and they come into room.)*

MRS. McCARTHY. Now, girls, this here is Miss Smith—

LULU ANN. Oh, just call me "Lulu Ann," ma'am —everybody does.

MRS. McCARTHY. Lulu Ann. She just came to our big city from away down in Dixie, didn't you, dearie?

LULU ANN. Uh-huh! Pikesboro, Alabama. I don't reckon any of you-all ever heard of it, did you? *(They* ALL *shake their heads.)* No, I reckon not, but it's a nice little place just the same. *(Laughs.)*

MRS. McCARTHY. Now, girls, we want to show Lulu Ann that the South hasn't got a monopoly on hospitality. As I was telling you, dearie, this isn't an ordinary boarding house; as long as you're in the big city you can think of Mrs. McCarthy's as your home and your club. We all try to be just one happy family here.

LULU ANN. Oh, yes, ma'am, I'm sure of that.

MRS. McCARTHY. Now, first I want you to meet Phyllis Deering—

LULU ANN. So happy to make your acquaintance.

PHYLLIS. Charmed.

MRS. McCARTHY. Phyllis is a big newspaper

woman—has one of the important jobs on the *Chronicle*.

LULU ANN. *(Awed)* My! Are you really a newspaper woman—a *reporter?*

PHYLLIS. Yes—in a way.

LULU ANN. Just think of that!

MRS. McCARTHY. And right over here is Arlene Day—

LULU ANN. So happy to make your acquaintance.

MRS. McCARTHY. Arlene's in business; she has one of the important jobs over at Himmelberger's. Of course you've heard of Himmelberger's Department Store.

LULU ANN. No-o. I can't rightly say I have. But it sounds important. *(Laughs)* I guess you must be one of those big business women I've been reading about.

ARLENE. Big? Why, Hon, hordes of women just fight to see me every day in the week.

LULU ANN. *(Wide-eyed)* Really?

MRS. McCARTHY. And this is Selena Barnes. She's with Wilde's, the big catering people.

LULU ANN. So happy to make your acquaintance!

SELENA. Come up and thee uth thome time. Thirty-five thent table de hotes our thpecialty.

LULU ANN. Oh, thank you ever so much.

MRS. McCARTHY. Now come over here, dearie, and shake hands with Claudia Vandermeer.

LULU ANN. So happy to make your acquaintance.

CLAUDIA. *(Stifling a yawn)* How'ja do?

LULU ANN. I'm fine. And what do you do, ma'am? Are you a business woman, too?

CLAUDIA. Heavens, no! I'm just a simple little home girl, doncha know. Nothing to do but loll around and try to entertain myself.

LULU ANN. My, I certainly envy that.

CLAUDIA. Hand me the cushion from that chair, won't you, girlie?

LULU ANN. Certainly. *(Gets a cushion from the chair down L. and hands it to her. CLAUDIA takes it and settles back in a thoroughly bored attitude.)*

ROSIE. *(Enters C. from R.)* Der room is all fixed up vonce, Mrs. McCarthy.

MRS. McCARTHY. All right, Rosie. You go downstairs and finish up in the kitchen.

ROSIE. Yah, I go. *(Exits C. to L.)*

MRS. McCARTHY. Now, as I was saying, dearie, this is not merely a boarding house. We have a heart here. You'll find us willing to extend a helping hand at all times. Once you live at Mrs. McCarthy's, dearie, you'll always call it home. Won't she, girls? *(They don't answer.)* Yes, indeed, the only reason I run a house like this is because I enjoy having the girls around me—helping them out when they need it. Because if I depended on the money it brought in, I'd be in the poorhouse in no time—the way some people *forget* to pay their bills. *(Looks at OTHERS significantly.)*

LULU ANN. Oh, would you like me to pay you now, Mrs. McCarthy?

MRS. McCARTHY. No, no hurry—whenever it's convenient, dearie. *(Extends her hand)* Twelve dollars a week—in advance.

LULU ANN. Certainly. *(Opens purse and hands her some bills)* Here you are, ma'am. I'll pay you for two weeks now. *(Laughs)* Because if I don't get a job, I don't know how long my money will hold out, and I'd rather you had it than somebody else.

MRS. McCARTHY. *(Pocketing the money)* I'll make out a receipt for you later.

SELENA. Thay, if you're job hunting, you might try Wilde's—that ith if you don't mind waiting on tableth for ten dollarth a week and tipth—and no tipth.

LULU ANN. That's *awfully* kind of you, ma'am,

but that isn't—it isn't exactly the kind of job I'm hunting.

ARLENE. Oh, she's particular.

LULU ANN. Oh, no, ma'am, it isn't that, but I— (Sets her chin defiantly) Well, I came up here to go on the stage and I'm going to get a job as an actress, ma'am, or bust.

MRS. MCCARTHY. An actress? Well, well, that's fine, dearie. You'll have to have a talk with Ray Cartwright.

LULU ANN. Who's that, ma'am?

MRS. MCCARTHY. Another one of our girls. She's had years of experience on the stage—very important parts, too. I'm sure she'll be glad to extend a helping hand.

LULU ANN. Oh, do you really think she would?

MRS. MCCARTHY. Certainly, certainly! She'll probably be able to get you something right off. Where is Ray, girls?

ARLENE. Out—hunting a job.

MRS. MCCARTHY. Oh. Well, she'll be back for dinner, and I'll introduce you, dearie.

PHYLLIS. What makes you think you'd be suited to the stage, Lulu Ann? Had any experience?

LULU ANN. Oh, yes, ma'am—loads of it. In the high school, you know—I was always in the plays we gave down there. Then the Little Theater—maybe you wouldn't believe it, but Pikesboro has one of the finest Little Theaters in the entire State of Alabama.

ARLENE. No! The entire State of Alabama!

LULU ANN. Uh-huh, that's honestly the truth, ma'am. The last play we gave in the Pikesboro Little Theater was *Macbeth*—that's by William Shakespeare. And I played the part of *Lady Macbeth*— You know, she's the one who walks in her sleep— And everyone sort of took one look at me and said

I ought to be on Broadway— *(Laughs)* I don't like to brag, but that's what they said.

PHYLLIS. I'm afraid you'll find Broadway quite a little different than Pikesboro, Alabama, Lulu Ann.

LULU ANN. Oh, I know that— I didn't exactly expect to find it any bed of roses. But I'll manage somehow. I've got to.

ARLENE. Sure, Hon, you'll manage. There's only about two million other girls who feel the same way you do.

LULU ANN. *(Determinedly)* I'll manage. Everyone said I would, and I will. You just wait and see, ma'am.

MRS. McCARTHY. Of course you will, dearie. A nice, bright girl like you. And you stop trying to discourage her, girls. (PHYLLIS *shrugs; opens one of her books; begins reading.)*

ARLENE. I don't want to discourage her, but if she's smart she'll grab that job Selena was speaking about at ten dollars per.

MRS. McCARTHY. Nonsense! You can always do what you really make up your mind to do.

LULU ANN. Yes, ma'am. That's the way I feel about it.

MRS. McCARTHY. That's the way the first Mr. McCarthy felt about it. If he hadn't, he wouldn't be where he is today.

LULU ANN. Where is he, ma'am?

ARLENE. Dead.

MRS. McCARTHY. The first Mr. McCarthy was a diamond miner, dearie. When he said he was going to mine for diamonds in Mexico, everyone laughed at him, said it couldn't be done. But he made up his mind there were diamonds there, and there were. Of course he did pass on of yellow fever he contracted down there, but if it hadn't been for his will power and his determination, he never would have left me the McCarthy Collection—

LULU ANN. The McCarthy Collection?

MRS. MCCARTHY. Oh, didn't I tell you about that, dearie?

LULU ANN. No, ma'am.

ARLENE. Don't worry, Hon—she will. *(The* OTHERS *laugh.)*

MRS. MCCARTHY. Arlene is such a nice person to have around. She keeps the entire house in a good humor. *(Glares at her.)*

LULU ANN. Yes, ma'am. But what *is* the McCarthy Collection? I'm awfully interested.

MRS. MCCARTHY. It's a long story, dearie. Remind me about it when I've got lots of time.

LULU ANN. All rightie. I will.

MRS. MCCARTHY. Right now I'll show you to your room. Then, by the time you've washed up for dinner, maybe Ray Cartwright will be back and you can have a nice talk about the theater.

CLAUDIA. *(Casually)* If you like, I'll take you down some day and introduce you to Sam Lubert.

LULU ANN. *(Breathless) Sam Lubert?* Do you know *him,* ma'am?

CLAUDIA. Know him? Don't be sil. Sam and I are like that—been chumming around for years, doncha know. Oh, my, yes.

LULU ANN. And you'll introduce me to him?

CLAUDIA. Certainly. He frequently asks my advice about his shows. Glad to do it. Oh, be a good girl and hand me one of those magazines, won't you?

LULU ANN. Oh, yes, ma'am. *(Gets magazine and gives it to her)* You-all have been so kind to me, I just don't know what to say. I— *(TELEPHONE rings. The* OTHERS *make a rush for it.)*

MRS. MCCARTHY. Girls. *(Claps her hands for attention)* Girls! Please let us remember that we are ladies. *(Crosses to telephone and picks up receiver)* This is Mrs. McCarthy's boarding house for girls—

Miss Day?—Yes, I believe she is in. Hold the wire, please.

ARLENE. Halelujah! Maybe it's a date! *(Rushes to phone and speaks in sugary voice)* Hello-oh!— This is Arle-an— Who?—Looie?— *(Her face falls)* Oh, yeah— Yeah— Uh-huh— *(Carries on a pantomimic conversation during the following.)*

MRS. McCARTHY. Come along, dearie. You don't want to be late for dinner. We're having something especially nice tonight.

LULU ANN. All rightie. *(Picks up her bag and they exeunt C. to R.)*

ARLENE. *(In telephone)* Well, wait a minute, Looie— I'll ask her. *(Covers mouthpiece with her hand. Calls to SELENA)* Say, Hon! It's Looie—remember?

SELENA. Looie—the plumber'th athithtant?

ARLENE. Yeah, that's the one. He and his boy friend've got two tickets to the wrestling matches. They want to know if we'll go.

SELENA. The latht time they took uth to the movieth, they walked uth all the way downtown and back.

ARLENE. Can they help it if they like the exercise?

SELENA. But think of my feet, Arlene.

ARLENE. Think of sitting here all night and listening to the story of the McCarthy Collection.

CLAUDIA. If you're looking for a fourth, Arlene, I've the whole evening free, doncha know.

ARLENE. That's awfully sweet of you, Hon, but they want Selena—and they might be particular. *(CLAUDIA returns to her magazine.)*

SELENA. After all, a man'th a man. I'll go.

ARLENE. *(In telephone)* We'll go— Okay, about eight— G'bye. *(Hangs up and comes back in room)* It's nice being so popular, isn't it?

SELENA. Well, a plumber'th athithtant ithn't tho bad, Arlene. It might be worthe.

ARLENE. Sure, look what he's got to look forward to. But as you say, a man's a man—even Looie.

SELENA. I thuppose we ought to change.

ARLENE. Yeah. I'll put on my three-ninety-eight special from Himmelberger's Basement. Come on, Hon. *(They cross to arch.)*

MRS. McCARTHY. *(Entering c. from r.)* Don't go far, girls. Dinner will be ready any minute.

ARLENE. Yeah. Save us a nice outside cut of the hash if we're late, will you? *(Exeunt c. to r.)*

MRS. McCARTHY. She's a nice little girl, isn't she, Phyllis?

PHYLLIS. *(Looking up from her book)* I beg your pardon?

MRS. McCARTHY. I said that little Lulu Ann is a nice girl, isn't she?

CLAUDIA. She seems a little small-townish, doncha know.

PHYLLIS. She's a nice enough kid, I guess. But I hate to see her bucking a tough street like Broadway. She's liable to get bruised.

MRS. McCARTHY. Now don't worry about that. I'll take care of her. I believe in protecting my girls, and they always know they can turn to me in their hour of need. Claudia, has it slipped your mind that you owe me a week's rent?

CLAUDIA. Rent?

MRS. McCARTHY. Yes, rent. Rent—you know, what you're supposed to pay me for your room and board. Twelve dollars.

CLAUDIA. Oh, that. Now, isn't that strange?—I completely forgot about it, doncha know.

MRS. McCARTHY. That's what I thought. You girls have such short memories about those things.

CLAUDIA. I hope you're not worried.

MRS. McCARTHY. Oh, no. But if you continue to forget, I'm liable not to remember that you're living here and lock the door some night before you get in.

(Stands there chattering away. PHYLLIS, *absorbed in her book, nods mechanically from time to time.)* Yes, as I was saying, Phyllis, nothing gives me greater pleasure than to extend a helping hand to a girl in need. And more than one I've helped up the ladder to success—not that I ask any credit for it, but— (MISS VERNE *enters* C. *from* L. *in street clothes and starts to cross past arch.)* Oh, Miss Verne!

MISS VERNE. *(Stops in arch)* Good evening.

MRS. McCARTHY. You're late, aren't you?

MISS VERNE. A little.

MRS. McCARTHY. And you weren't here for breakfast this morning, were you?

MISS VERNE. No.

MRS. McCARTHY. Come to think of it, I didn't see you for dinner last night.

MISS VERNE. That's right.

MRS. McCARTHY. *(Laughs)* Guess I'll have to give you a rebate on your board bill.

MISS VERNE. I guess you will.

MRS. McCARTHY. Seriously, Miss Verne, you shouldn't keep yourself such a stranger. You've been in my house two weeks now, and I don't believe I've spoken six words to you.

MISS VERNE. Oh, I wouldn't say that.

MRS. McCARTHY. You ought to mix more with the others. We've got some very nice girls here, haven't we, Phyllis? I'm sure you'd find them very interesting.

MISS VERNE. I'm sure I would.

MRS. McCARTHY. Well, I guess you've been pretty busy, haven't you?

MISS VERNE. Yes, I have.

MRS. McCARTHY. As the first Mr. McCarthy always used to say, you've got to keep your nose to the grindstone if you want to get anywhere in this world.

I don't believe I remember what line you told me
you were in, Miss Verne.

MISS VERNE. I don't believe I ever told you, Mrs.
McCarthy.

MRS. McCARTHY. Didn't you? Now, isn't that
funny?

MISS VERNE. Yes, isn't it? Now, if you'll excuse
me, I'd really like to wash up.

MRS. McCARTHY. Don't be late for dinner.

MISS VERNE. I won't. *(Exits c. to r.)*

MRS. McCARTHY. *(Stands in arch watching her
off)* There's a cool customer if ever I saw one.

PHYLLIS. She doesn't have much to say, does she?

MRS. McCARTHY. She's as close-mouthed as a
cigar-store Indian. You mark my words, that girl is
up to some mischief.

PHYLLIS. Oh, Mrs. McCarthy! You don't know
anything about her.

MRS. McCARTHY. I know what I see, and it gives
me the shudders just to look at her. You be careful
of your belongings as long as she's around, girls.
The first Mr. McCarthy always said I was the best
judge of human nature he ever knew, and I had her
sized up the minute I laid eyes on her. Wasn't going to give her the room at all, but she offered me a
whole month in advance, and of course—

PHYLLIS. Yes, of course.

MRS. McCARTHY. The thin lips on her, and the
way her eyes are set so far apart. I don't mind telling you she's got me worried—wish I knew what
she was up to. And I better tell Rosie to keep an eye
on the silver—

LULU ANN. *(Enters c. from r.)* Am I late?

MRS. McCARTHY. No, dearie—but Rosie is. That
girl—she needs someone standing over her all the
time. Well, how do you like your room, dearie?

LULU ANN. Oh, it's gorgeous, ma'am, just gor-

geous. With a room like that, I'll just naturally have
to get me a big part in some fine play.

Mrs. McCarthy. Why, certainly you will. "The
man with the grin is the man who will win." That's
what the first Mr. McCarthy always used to say.

Lulu Ann. Did he, ma'am? Oh, I'm simply consumed with curiosity about the McCarthy Collection.

Mrs. McCarthy. Oh, that. Well, sit down,
dearie, and I'll tell you about it.

Lulu Ann. Thank you, ma'am. *(They sit together in the divan,* Claudia *ungraciously making
room for them.)*

Mrs. McCarthy. *(Leans over and lowers her
voice)* Now, this is strictly confidential, you understand. There's very, very few people who know anything about it, because I wouldn't want it to get out
that there's anything so valuable in the house.

Lulu Ann. Oh, I wouldn't tell a soul—cross my
heart and hope to die. *(The* Others *pay no attention, this apparently being an old story to them.)*

Mrs. McCarthy. All right. Well, the McCarthy
Collection is a group of the finest and purest uncut
diamonds that was ever mined on this continent.

Lulu Ann. No! Honestly?

Mrs. McCarthy. Yes. The first Mr. McCarthy
spent ten years of his life getting them together. If
I was ever to let you see them—

Lulu Ann. Oh, would you, ma'am? I love
diamonds—they're so pretty. Would you let me see
them?

Mrs. McCarthy. Well, I don't know about that.
If I was to tell you how much they're valued at—
They've been exhibited in all the best galleries in
the country. And once I was invited to Amsterdam
—that's in Europe, dearie—with all my expenses
paid, just to show them at the convention there.

Lulu Ann. My! I bet they must be simply gorgeous. And you keep them right here in this very house?

MRS. McCARTHY. I'm not saying I do. But you don't think I'd be fool enough to leave them any place I couldn't keep my eye on them? Anyway, they're insured for plenty, all right.

LULU ANN. Well, wouldn't you give me the teeniest weeniest peek at them, ma'am? I promise I wouldn't—

(RAY *enters* C. *from* L. *in street clothes. Tries to steal past arch to* R.)

MRS. McCARTHY. *(Sees* RAY *as latter is almost past)* Miss Cartwright! *(Rises.* LULU ANN *rises.)*

RAY. *(Comes back and stands in arch)* Good evening, Mrs. McCarthy. I'm sorry about the money. I thought I'd have it for you tonight, but—

MRS. McCARTHY. Never mind, we'll talk about that later. I want you to meet Lulu Ann Smith—she's coming to live with us. And this is Ray Cartwright, dearie.

RAY. How do you do?

LULU ANN. So happy to make your acquaintance.

MRS. McCARTHY. Ray is that famous actress I was telling you about.

LULU ANN. Uh-huh! And it's a big thrill for me just speaking to you, ma'am.

MRS. McCARTHY. Lulu Ann is thinking of going on the stage herself, and I told her you could probably give her some good advice.

RAY. I can. *(Turns and looks at* LULU ANN*)* Go home.

LULU ANN. *(Her face falls)* Oh, I—I'm sorry, ma'am, but I couldn't do that.

RAY. Why not? Haven't you got the fare?

LULU ANN. Yes, ma'am. It isn't that, but—

HANNAH. *(Bursts in* C. *from* R., *looking radiant*

in an evening gown) How do you think I look, Mrs. McCarthy?

MRS. MCCARTHY. Like all the king's horses, dearie. I want you to meet a new member of our family, Lulu Ann Smith—this is Hannah Williams.

LULU ANN. So happy to make your acquaintance! *(RAY crosses to window, stands with her back to the OTHERS and to the audience; holds a handkerchief to her face.)*

HANNAH. *(Gushing)* How do you do? I feel all fluttery, if you know what I mean. The most wonderful thing happened to me today—I can hardly think straight. It was so romantic—

LULU ANN. Honest? You're lucky.

HANNAH. I'll say I am. It must have been fate—it couldn't have been anything else. And he's calling for me at eight. *(Pivots around)* Do you think I look all right?

LULU ANN. Gorgeous—just gorgeous!

HANNAH. Sylvester Crookingham—don't you think it's the most romantic name? And you should see the adorable little mole under his chin— Wait till I tell you about it—

ROSIE. *(Enters C. from L.)* So! It's all ready, Mrs. McCarthy. Everything on the table is.

MRS. MCCARTHY. All right. I'll be right down.

ROSIE. Yah. *(Exits C. to L.)*

MRS. MCCARTHY. *(Steps into arch and calls off R.)* Dinner! Girls—dinner!

HANNAH. Oh, I've simply got to fly— I don't want to be late. I'll tell you all about it later—! *(Runs off C. to R.)*

PHYLLIS. *(Rises; sniffs the air)* I get the fragrant aroma of the McCarthy hash all the way up here. *(Exits C. to L.)*

CLAUDIA. I feel so exhausted, doncha know, Mrs. McCarthy—couldn't you manage to have a tray sent up for me? (ARLENE *and* SELENA *rush past arch* C. *from* R. *and off to* L.)

MRS. McCARTHY. I most certainly could not. You know the rules of this house as well as I do, Claudia —and I never make exceptions.

CLAUDIA. Oh, very well. But I don't know how I'll ever get downstairs. *(To* LULU ANN*)* Be a good girl and give me a hand, will you?

LULU ANN. Certainly. *(Helps her up from divan.* GRAYCE *crosses past arch* C. *from* R. *and off to* L.)

CLAUDIA. Thanks-loads. Oh, dear! *(Smothers a yawn and languidly exits* C. *to* L.)

MRS. McCARTHY. Come on, dearie. First helping is always best, you know.

LULU ANN. All rightie. *(Starts to exit, hesitates)* Aren't you coming, ma'am?

RAY. In a minute. I—I want to wash up first.

LULU ANN. Yes, ma'am. *(Follows* MRS. Mc-CARTHY *out* C. *to* L. RAY *crosses, sinks down in divan and begins to weep quietly, her head on her arms. After a few moments* LULU ANN *re-enters* C. *from* L. *She approaches* RAY *shyly)* Ahum! *(Clears her throat.)*

RAY. *(Starts)* Oh! I—I thought you went down to dinner.

LULU ANN. Yes, ma'am, I did. But I noticed you weren't feeling very well, and I thought—

RAY. That's kind of you, but I'll be all right. I'm just—just a little tired.

LULU ANN. Isn't there anything I can do—anything at all?

RAY. No, my dear, I'm afraid there isn't.

LULU ANN. Maybe you'll think I'm being awfully cheeky for suggesting this, ma'am, but—well, if it's a question of money, I've got quite a little saved up and I—

RAY. *(Protestingly)* Please—

LULU ANN. I know it's none of my business,

ma'am, but I heard what you said to Mrs. McCarthy about the money, and I think it's an awful shame— a person who's been as famous as you and all—

RAY. Let's just forget the whole thing, shall we?

LULU ANN. Well, yes, ma'am—if you want me to.

RAY. I do. It's nice of you taking an interest in an old has-been like me—

LULU ANN. Oh, don't say that, ma'am. You're not old, and I'm sure you're not a has-been. Why, I feel like a cheeky little upstart even daring to speak to you.

RAY. You shouldn't. You're a very sweet girl, Lulu Ann—is that your name?

LULU ANN. Yes, ma'am—Lulu Ann Smith.

RAY. It's a pretty name. (Looks at her with more interest. Smiles) And so you want to be an actress?

LULU ANN. Yes, ma'am.

RAY. You think you'd really like to be like—like me?

LULU ANN. I'd be proud to, ma'am. It's what I want—what I've always wanted—more than anything in the world, ever since I can remember.

RAY. Yes, I think I know that feeling. And I suppose nothing I nor anyone else could say would possibly discourage you.

LULU ANN. I'm afraid not, ma'am. At least not until I've tried and found out for myself.

RAY. Yes, I suppose you'll have to. I suppose you'll have to try your wings—to experience the same heartaches, disappointments, defeats, perhaps little triumphs—I suppose you'll have to go through the mill as we all do. But believe me, and I know what I'm speaking about, my dear—it isn't worth it.

LULU ANN. I wish you wouldn't speak that way, Miss Cartwright. Because, whatever you say, I'm just going to have to try it for myself.

RAY. Why are you so determined?

LULU ANN. Well, ma'am, it's partly for the sake of the folks back home.

RAY. They think you can act?

LULU ANN. They're sure of it, and don't you see how foolish I'd feel if I went back there without even trying?

RAY. And how about your folks?

LULU ANN. I haven't any, ma'am. I live with my grandfather back there. He's the nicest, kindest old gentleman, ma'am—I wish you could meet him.

RAY. Oh, yes. I'd like to. *(Sighs)* Well, if you're foolish enough to want to enter the most heartless, competitive business in the world, I suppose there's nothing left for me to do but help you.

LULU ANN. *(Overjoyed)* Oh, ma'am! Would you —honestly?

RAY. *(Smiles)* Just how much do you know about acting? You can't have had much experience.

LULU ANN. Oh, but I have—loads and loads of it.

RAY. Really?

LULU ANN. Uh-huh. I played *Juliet,* and *Desdemona,* and *Joan of Arc,* and *Salome*—

RAY. Dear me! All that—at your age?

LULU ANN. Yes, ma'am—in the Pikesboro Little Theatre. It's one of the finest in—

RAY. *(In a voice suddenly cold) Where?*

LULU ANN. Pikesboro, ma'am—Pikesboro, Alabama. I don't suppose you've ever been there?

RAY. *(After a pause)* No. *(Rises and crosses to window)* No, I've never been there.

LULU ANN. Hardly anyone has. But you'd be surprised at the things we do in the Little Theater. In Alabama it has the reputation of being—

(WARN Curtain.)

RAY. *(Crosses back to her; takes her by the shoulders)* What did you say your name is?

LULU ANN. Why—Lulu Ann Smith, ma'am.

RAY. *(Tensely)* You're sure—sure of that?

LULU ANN. Of course. It's my own name, ma'am. *(RAY stands there, staring into her eyes.)* Why are you staring at me like that, Miss Cartwright?

RAY. *(Lets go of her)* Was I? I'm sorry. It's my— I have a little headache. *(Crosses away from her.)*

LULU ANN. Oh, can't I get you something?

RAY. No, no. I—it's really—

ROSIE. *(Entering* C. *from* L.*)* Excuse, please. Mrs. McCarthy, she say you better come down. Everything it's getting cold yet.

RAY. Yes, we're coming.

ROSIE. Yah.

RAY. Come on, child. We—we don't want everything to get cold, do we?

LULU ANN. *(Looks at her curiously)* No, ma'am. I guess not. *(They exeunt* C. *to* L.*, followed by* ROSIE.*)*

MISS VERNE. *(Enters, after a moment,* C. *from* R. *Looks into the room, satisfying herself no one is there. Goes back into arch and looks off* L. *Then she strides over to telephone and dials a number. She begins to speak in low tones, glancing about her apprehensively all through the conversation)* Hello, that you, Chief?—This is—you know who— Listen, I haven't got much time, but I think I've located the stuff— Yeah, they're in the house, all right— The chance will come any time now, and I'm going to be right here when it does—

CURTAIN

ACT TWO

THE TIME: *Several days later. Sunday. Late in the morning.*

THE PLACE: *The same.*

AT RISE: ARLENE, SELENA *and* GRAYCE *are discovered. Sections of the Sunday paper are scattered everywhere around the room.* ARLENE *and* SELENA *are sprawled on the floor* C. *with the "funnies."* PHYLLIS *is seated in the divan reading a book.*

ARLENE. The Inspector gets it in the neck again.

SELENA. Poor little Inspector. I feel tho thorry for him, don't you?

ARLENE. Yeah, my heart bleeds for him. You through?

SELENA. Uh-huh! Let'th turn over. *(They turn the page.)*

ARLENE. Ah, Jiggs! Is he going to put it over on Maggie?

SELENA. He never doeth, but let'th thee.

PHYLLIS. Quiet, you two! How can I concentrate?

ARLENE. You and Grayce, always concentrating! Why don't you relax for a change, Hon?

SELENA. Ith it a good book, Phil?

PHYLLIS. Grand! I'm right in the midst of the seventh murder.

SELENA. Oh, my, it mutht be thrilling.

37

PHYLLIS. You know, I think I've discovered the secret of writing these things.

ARLENE. What is it, Hon?

PHYLLIS. Well, you start off at about sixty miles an hour, and keep increasing the speed as you go along.

ARLENE. Sounds easy.

ROSIE. *(Enters c. from l. Looks at room, shakes her head)* Ach! Such a messing up! Und I joost clean the room nice for Sunday. *(Begins gathering up the newspaper.)*

ARLENE. Go on, you wouldn't be happy if you didn't have something to do.

ROSIE. Yah? Dot I von't never know, because always it gives something.

ARLENE. Listen, Hon, what's the old gal so excited about this morning?

ROSIE. Old gel? *(Beams)* I know dot already— Mrs. McCarthy.

ARLENE. She's been bustling about acting so mysterious.

ROSIE. Yah, she goes somewhere vonce this afternoon.

ARLENE. Where?

ROSIE. Dot she don't tell me. She puts on her best clothes yet. It moost be important, yah?

SELENA. It thertainly mutht.

ROSIE. So. *(Places the papers in a neat pile on table c.)* Dot's much better already.

ARLENE. What did you do with the society section, Hon?

SELENA. I don't know. I gueth Rosie took it. *(ARLENE rises, crosses to the table, begins scattering the paper about looking for the society section.)*

ROSIE. Vait! Vait! Look yet vhat you're doing!

ARLENE. Now, be calm—that's what Sunday papers are for.

ROSIE. Ach! Such vork it gives in this house. I—

MRS. McCARTHY. *(Calling from off* R.*)* Ro-seee!

ROSIE. Der madame! *(Calls)* Yah, yah—I come! *(Rushes off* C. *to* R.*)*

ARLENE. *(Sits down* L. *with paper)* T'st, t'st!

SELENA. *(Rises; crosses to her)* What'th the matter?

ARLENE. I see where poor Mrs. Vanderfeller had to close up two of her country estates because of the rising cost of living. And we think *we* have troubles.

PHYLLIS. You will have if you don't quiet down, and that quickly. I've read this paragraph four times now, and I still don't know what it's about.

GRAYCE. *(Enters breezily* C. *from* R. *She is dressed for the street)* Good morning, Phyllis! Good morning, Arlene! Good morning, Selena! It's a lovely morning, isn't it?

ARLENE. What are you all hopped up about, Hon?

GRAYCE. *(Comes down* C. SELENA *sits in divan with* PHYLLIS*)* Look out that window. It's a grand spring morning. The sun is shining. When I awoke, a lark was singing on my sill—

ARLENE. *(Looks at her in alarm)* Hon! What's wrong with you? Do you want a doctor?

GRAYCE. Nothing is wrong. Everything is right.

ARLENE. Yeah, that's what worries me. I've never seen you this way before.

PHYLLIS. *(Looks up from her book)* Let us in on the good news, Grayce.

GRAYCE. You're right, Phyllis—I have had good news. I'm going to be able to give my concert very soon.

PHYLLIS. Well, congratulations!

GRAYCE. *(Exuberantly)* Thank you—thank you! Oh, isn't it marvelous, girls?

ARLENE. Swell, Hon!

SELENA. It'th grand, Grayth. I'm tho glad for your thake.

PHYLLIS. When's it to be?

GRAYCE. The end of the month. You'll all be there, of course, to see me make my debut.

PHYLLIS. Of course. I wouldn't miss it for anything.

GRAYCE. "Grayce Johnston, the eminent pianist, in a recital of—" Oh, I'm so thrilled I can barely speak.

PHYLLIS. It may be the beginning of a great career.

GRAYCE. It's a chance, at any rate—*my* chance— what I've been waiting for. *(Smiles rapturously, lost in her thoughts.)*

ARLENE. Pardon the curiosity, Hon, but where did you get the five hundred?

GRAYCE. All my life I've looked forward to this moment. Ever since I can— What? What did you say, Arlene?

ARLENE. I said where'd you get the wherewithal, Hon—the dough-ray-me?

GRAYCE. *(Her mood suddenly changing)* I— Well, I just got it. *(Bites her lips nervously.)*

ARLENE. Rich uncle die and leave you a million?

GRAYCE. *(Curtly)* Really, Arlene, I don't care to discuss it.

ARLENE. Oops! Pardon me.

GRAYCE. *(Crosses to arch)* And I really must be going. I have an appointment with the concert manager at twelve. Excuse me! *(Exits, testily, C. to L. The GIRLS exchange glances.)*

ARLENE. Did I say something?

SELENA. I don't think she liked your athking her about the money.

ARLENE. Well, after all, where *did* she get it?

PHYLLIS. She's been saving up for it a long time.

ARLENE. Only the other day she was telling us she'd never make it on her salary of eighteen dollars per week. Remember, Hon?

SELENA. Yeth, that'th what she thaid.

ARLENE. She's certainly acting funny about it.

PHYLLIS. *(Returns to her book)* After all, it's no concern of ours where she got it.

ARLENE. Nope. No skin off my back. *(Starts reading her paper.)*

SELENA. Wathn't Looie thuppoosed to call uth today, Arlene?

ARLENE. If he doesn't forget, and it'll be just our luck he won't. I've still got black and blue marks on my arms from the last date.

PHYLLIS. Sounds like quite a cave man.

ARLENE. It's not that, Hon. We went to the wrestling matches, and Looie put his whole heart and soul into it. Every time one of the wrestlers would grunt, Looie'd start beating a tattoo on my arms. Honest, I suffered more than anyone in the ring—only I didn't get paid for it.

SELENA. And then, after the matcheth, they inthithted on taking uth for a long walk. Can you imagine—*me?*

PHYLLIS. *(Smiles)* Sort of like carrying coals to Newcastle.

SELENA. Uh-huh! Out of about five million men in thith town, I would have to get a walking enthuthiatht.

ARLENE. You're the one who said "A man's a man," Hon.

SELENA. I've changed my mind. They're not men —they're perpetual motion machineth.

RAY. *(Enters* c. *from* r. *Stands in arch)* Hello! May I come in?

PHYLLIS. Certainly. Come on and sit with me, Ray. *(Makes room for her on the divan.)*

RAY. Thank you. *(Crosses and sits down.)*

PHYLLIS. How are you these days? Feeling all right?

RAY. Oh, yes—thank you.

PHYLLIS. What's the latest around the theaters?

RAY. I wouldn't know, my dear. I haven't been in one so long—except as a spectator.

PHYLLIS. Well, cheer up. Things are bound to improve.

RAY. Oh, I'm not complaniing. I'll get something one of these days, I'm sure.

PHYLLIS. Of course you will. And how's that little girl—what's her name—Lulu Ann? *(Smiles)* Has she become a great star yet?

RAY. *(Rather abruptly)* I don't know.

PHYLLIS. Well, wasn't she sort of a protege of yours?

RAY. No. *(Changing the subject)* Isn't it a lovely day?

ARLENE. *(Rising)* Yeah. Come on, Hon—we've seen all the paper. Let's get a little air.

SELENA. *(Rises)* All right, but pothitively no walking.

ARLENE. We'll sit on the front porch and wait for something to happen. Maybe that Prince Charming of yours will turn up.

SELENA. I thertainly hope tho. *(Exeunt C. to L.)*

RAY. Have you started to write that new book of yours yet, dear?

PHYLLIS. Not yet. But I'm completely saturated in the technique. I believe I could qualify easily as an expert on murders.

RAY. Let's hope you'll never have to do that.

MRS. McCARTHY. *(Entering C. from R.)* Hello, hello! Where's everybody? Oh, have you seen Lulu Ann, Phyllis? *(She is wearing an elaborate but slightly old-fashioned gown and bustles about importantly.)*

PHYLLIS. Not recently. She's probably in her room.

MRS. McCARTHY. Oh! Rosie! Where's Rosie? That girl—she's never—

PHYLLIS. Why, she went to your room when you called her a while ago, Mrs. McCarthy.

MRS. McCARTHY. Yes, I know, but I sent her to look for my lace scarf, and she hasn't got it yet. *(At arch, calls)* Ro-seee!

RAY. *(Rises)* I wanted to talk to you, Mrs. McCarthy.

MRS. McCARTHY. I'm awfully busy, but—what about?

RAY. Well, it's about that money I owe.

MRS. McCARTHY. Money? What money?

RAY. My rent. Four weeks, isn't it?

MRS. McCARTHY. It's been paid.

RAY. Paid? I don't understand. I didn't pay it.

MRS. McCARTHY. Of course you didn't. But some-one else did.

RAY. Who?

MRS. McCARTHY. Someone in the house. They didn't want me to tell you.

RAY. But if someone paid my rent, Mrs. McCarthy, I think—

MRS. McCARTHY. I'm too busy to argue with you, Ray. It's been paid, so stop worrying about it.

RAY. But I—I— *(Stands there, not knowing what to say.)*

MRS. McCARTHY. Where is that girl? *(Calls again)* Ro-seee!

PHYLLIS. I gather you have an important engage-ment this afternoon.

MRS. McCARTHY. Important? Well, it certainly is. It's the most important— (ROSIE *enters* C. *from* R., *carrying a scarf)* Oh, Rosie, haven't you got that scarf yet?

ROSIE. Yah, here it is. *(Hands it to her.)*

MRS. McCARTHY. All right. *(Takes it; wraps it around her throat)* Now help me fasten it.

ROSIE. *(Secures it with a clip)* So, it's fixed.

MRS. McCARTHY. *(Fussing with it)* Does it look all right, Phyllis?

PHYLLIS. Fine.

ROSIE. You vant me to get der lunch ready vonce?

MRS. McCARTHY. Yes, of course— No! Ask Miss Smith—Lulu Ann Smith—if she can come in here first.

ROSIE. Yah, I ask her. *(Bustles out c. to R.)*

MRS. McCARTHY. I know I'll never be ready— What time is it—? I can't seem to do anything right today— And if I'm late—

PHYLLIS. Where are you going?

MRS. McCARTHY. Where am I going? *(Looks around. Then, in a loud whisper)* The McCarthy Collection!

PHYLLIS. Oh! Another exhibition?

MRS. McCARTHY. Not just another exhibition. *(In tone of deepest secrecy)* Don't tell a soul. It may be the most important thing that ever happened in my life.

PHYLLIS. Well, that's nice, isn't it?

MRS. McCARTHY. *(Sighs)* If only the first Mr. McCarthy could be here to share my triumph. Well, dear me, dear me—I mustn't live in the past. I have things to do—so many things—

ROSIE. *(Re-enters c. from R.)* She be right in, soon. (RAY *frowns; seems visibly affected by this information.)*

MRS. McCARTHY. All right. Well, don't stand there, Rosie. Get busy on your lunch. You're going to be late.

ROSIE. Yah. Ach, so many things it gives to do in this house yet. *(Exits c. to L.)*

RAY. *(Crosses to arch)* Excuse me, won't you—?

MRS. McCARTHY. I'd like you to stay in here, Ray.

RAY. Why?

MRS. McCARTHY. I can't tell you now, but you just stay in this room a few minutes longer.

RAY. *(Reluctantly)* Well—all right, if you want me to. *(Crosses and sits down L.)*

MRS. McCARTHY. Yes, indeed, Phyllis, if what I think is going to happen today does happen, it will give me the opportunity I have always wanted.

PHYLLIS. What opportunity is that?

MRS. McCARTHY. The opportunity to help my girls—to do some good in this world. As the first Mr. McCarthy used to say to me, "Mazie, you've got a heart as big as a watermelon." Of course, I've always tried to do my share to the best of my ability, but this— *(Leans over and whispers with an air of great importance)* This is something big.

PHYLLIS. Well—

MRS. McCARTHY. No, don't ask me to tell you any more, Phyllis. I have been pledged to secrecy. However, if you promise not to breathe a word, I'll tell you this much— (HANNAH *enters* C. *from* R.) Sshh! Come in, dearie.

HANNAH. Hello, everybody! Oh, Phil, my white gloves have a hole in them that big, and they're the only pair I've got, and—

PHYLLIS. You can have mine, if they'll fit. They're on top of my dresser.

HANNAH. *(Flutters)* Thanks *awfully,* Phil. I must fly— I haven't a single moment—

PHYLLIS. Seeing Sylvester today?

HANNAH. Yes, I am—and I'm late now. I've simply got to fly—

PHYLLIS. Well, go ahead and fly—don't let me keep you.

HANNAH. Yes, I must. *(Crosses to arch)* Oh, gosh, it's the most romantic thing—I wish I could tell you—guess where we're going?

PHYLLIS. I haven't the vaguest idea.

HANNAH. We're going over to Jersey—to the Westmore Livery Stables.

PHYLLIS. Livery stables—?

HANNAH. Uh-huh. It's just about the largest stable in the world, and there isn't a single veterinarian who wouldn't give his right eye to get their practice, and Sylvester thinks he's got the inside track on it. Isn't it *romantic?*

PHYLLIS. Oh, yes—yes, indeed.

HANNAH. I've simply got to fly— I wouldn't want to miss it for anything in the world.

LULU ANN. *(Entering C. from R.)* Hello, you-all.

HANNAH. Oh, hello, Lulu Ann. I was just telling everyone about the most *marvelous* thing that happened to Sylvester—

LULU ANN. Well, I'm right glad to hear that, Hannah.

HANNAH. So romantic! But I haven't a single minute. I must— Oh, thanks, Phil dear— I'll take the gloves.

PHYLLIS. All right.

HANNAH. G'bye now! *(Flies out C. to R.)*

MRS. MCCARTHY. That girl can swallow her breath faster than anyone I know.

LULU ANN. *(To MRS. MCCARTHY)* Rosie said you wanted me, ma'am.

MRS. MCCARTHY. I did, dearie. You just stay right here, and I'll be back in a minute.

LULU ANN. All rightie! (MRS. MCCARTHY *exits* C. *to* R.)

PHYLLIS. Any luck on Broadway yet, Lulu Ann? (RAY *rises; starts pacing back and forth.)*

LULU ANN. Well—nothing definite I don't guess you'd say, ma'am—but I have got a lot of good prospects.

PHYLLIS. Well, that's fine. Just keep at it.

LULU ANN. Oh, I intend to. Why, there was one place I almost got a part last Friday.

PHYLLIS. Really?

LULU ANN. Uh-huh! The man was *awfully* nice to me, ma'am. He asked me to read something for him, and I did, and he told me to come back the next day.

PHYLLIS. What happened when you went back?

LULU ANN. Oh, the man sent out word it wasn't any use seeing me because he already had someone else for the part, but I think it's awfully encouraging getting so far, don't you, ma'am?

PHYLLIS. Oh, yes—awfully encouraging.

LULU ANN. Because, after all, Rome wasn't built in a day, was it, ma'am? *(Laughs. To* RAY*)* Is something wrong, Miss Cartwright? Don't you feel well?

RAY. *(Curtly)* I feel all right.

LULU ANN. Well—I just thought I'd ask, ma'am.

RAY. I appreciate that. *(Nervously)* Where is Mrs. McCarthy? What does she want me in here for?

LULU ANN. Me, too. I'm simply consumed with curiosity.

PHYLLIS. Yes, she likes to keep people guessing.

LULU ANN. Oh, Miss Cartwright, we just don't seem to have had much chance to see much of each other since that first night, have we?

RAY. Haven't we?

LULU ANN. You just don't seem to be around when I'm here, ma'am, and I guess when I'm out, you're here.

RAY. I hadn't noticed particularly.

LULU ANN. Oh, hadn't you? What I mean is— well, you promised to help me, sort of, if you remember, ma'am, and I thought—

RAY. I'm sorry. I—I've been busy.

LULU ANN. Yes, ma'am, I reckon you have

RAY. It's all I can do to take care of my own

affairs, without having to worry about someone else's.

LULU ANN. *(Hurt)* Oh, I—I'm right sorry, Miss Cartwright. I didn't know. I certainly wouldn't want to interfere— (PHYLLIS *takes in this conversation, finding something unusual in* RAY'S *attitude.)*

RAY. The only way I can help you is by telling you again what I told you the first time I saw you: Go home to Kentucky, or wherever it is—

LULU ANN. *(Not far from tears)* Alabama, ma'am—Pikesboro, Alabama.

RAY. Yes. Well, whatever it is—that's still my advice to you: go back.

LULU ANN. Th-thank you, ma'am—thank you very much indeed. I— *(Turns and rushes to arch. Stops there.)*

PHYLLIS. Lulu Ann, come here and sit down with me. I'm sure Ray didn't mean to—

LULU ANN. No, it's all right, ma'am. I understand.

HANNAH. *(Enters to arch,* C. *from* R., *completely dressed for the street and carrying a pair of white gloves)* Here I am again, kids. Oh, I found your gloves, Phil. *(Waves them at her.)*

PHYLLIS. I see you did.

HANNAH. I simply daren't linger another single moment— Wish us luck, kids—

LULU ANN. G-good luck.

HANNAH. Because if Sylvester makes this connection— Oh, it'll be too wonderful. Well, I'm off— G'bye, everybody, g'bye, g'bye! *(The others ad lib. "goodbyes" and she rushes off* C. *to* L. RAY *stands at the window, her back to the* OTHERS.)

PHYLLIS. *(Laughs, trying to cheer* LULU ANN) She certainly is a funny girl, isn't she?

LULU ANN. Yes, ma'am, she certainly is.

PHYLLIS. Have you been out today yet? It's so nice and— *(Suddenly, a loud, pie ng CRY is heard from off* R. *They start and jump to their feet.)*

LULU ANN. My heavens! What's that—?

PHYLLIS. Sounds awful— *(Again the SCREAM is heard.)*

RAY. It's Mrs. McCarthy. *(They rush to the arch.)*

MRS. McCARTHY. *(From off* R.*)* Help! Help!

PHYLLIS. *(Looking off* R.*)* Mrs. McCarthy—what is it? What's the matter?

MRS. McCARTHY. *(Staggers on* C. *from* R., *looking as if the world were at an end)* Oohh! Help—!

PHYLLIS. *(Taking her by shoulders)* Mrs. McCarthy, what is it? What's the matter? Tell us what happened.

MRS. McCARTHY. *(Moaning incoherently)* It's terrible, terrible—! Oh, my Lord, what'll I do, what'll I do—?

LULU ANN. What is it, ma'am? Did someone harm you?

MRS. McCARTHY. The McCarthy Collection—

PHYLLIS. Good heavens! What about it?

MRS. McCARTHY. Gone—it's gone! What'll I do now—?

LULU ANN. You mean someone stole your diamonds, ma'am?

MRS. McCARTHY. Gone. They're stolen. I'm a poor woman now—the McCarthy Collection stolen!

LULU ANN. Oh, that's terrible! Maybe the thief is still in the house. Maybe we can find him—let's all look—

PHYLLIS. I'm afraid that would be useless, Lulu Ann.

LULU ANN. But can't we do something, ma'am? Poor Mrs. McCarthy—

MRS. McCARTHY. I'm a poor woman. They're gone—gone—

PHYLLIS. We can't do anything until we get the facts. Come on, now—you'll have to tell us what happened. Sit down here. *(Guides her to divan and sits her down.)*

MRS. McCARTHY. I'm a poor woman. Everything I had in the world is gone—gone—

PHYLLIS. I'm sure it's not as bad as that. The diamonds were insured, weren't they?

MRS. McCARTHY. Only for a fraction of what they're worth. I won't get anything, hardly. I'm ruined. Oohhh!

ARLENE. *(Rushes on C. from L. with SELENA)* What's all the commotion?

SELENA. We heard the motht awful thcreamth—

LULU ANN. Someone stole poor Mrs. McCarthy's diamonds, ma'am.

ARLENE. What! The McCarthy Collection—?

MRS. McCARTHY. Gone! Everything I owned in the world—

SELENA. Graciouth!

ARLENE. How did it happen, Hon?

MRS. McCARTHY. I don't know. I don't know. All I know is that they're gone—my diamonds—the McCarthy Collection. I can't understand it— What would the first Mr. McCarthy say if he knew I'd lost his diamonds? I've got to get them back—I've got to!

PHYLLIS. Perhaps we can help you, if you'll tell us all the facts—everything.

RAY. I believe the police should be called, Phyllis.

ARLENE. They certainly should. Hasn't anybody called them yet?

MRS. McCARTHY. Yes, yes—the police. Call them. And the insurance company. You don't understand. I've got to get my diamonds back. Call them, please.

ARLENE. I'll do it, Hon. What's the name of the insurance company?

MRS. McCARTHY. The Grand Mutual.

ARLENE. Grand Mutual. Right. *(Crosses toward telephone.)*

PHYLLIS. Wait a minute, Arlene.

ARLENE. *(Stops in arch)* Yeah?

PHYLLIS. Mrs. McCarthy, what are you interested in most right now?

MRS. McCARTHY. Only one thing—getting my diamonds back.

PHYLLIS. All right! Then if you want them back, I advise you not to get the police in—not yet.

ARLENE. But, Hon—

PHYLLIS. Just a minute, Arlene. Mrs. McCarthy, where did you keep those diamonds?

MRS. McCARTHY. *(Hesitates)* Well, I—I don't know that I should—

PHYLLIS. Very well, I won't press that point just yet. But they were somewhere in this house?

MRS. McCARTHY. *(Short pause)* Yes.

PHYLLIS. Then has it occurred to you that it must have been an inside job?

MRS. McCARTHY. Oh, but—you mean one of my girls would do a thing like that to me?

PHYLLIS. When did you see them last?

MRS. McCARTHY. Only last night. I looked at them just before I went to sleep.

PHYLLIS. And there hasn't been anyone in the house between last night and now, has there—any stranger?

MRS. McCARTHY. I don't know—I don't know. I can't think of anyone.

RAY. Phyllis is quite right. If there had been anyone, one of us would have noticed.

PHYLLIS. Exactly. It appears, Mrs. McCarthy, that one of your "dear girls" is a thief.

ARLENE. I don't see what that's got to do with having the police in.

PHYLLIS. Just this, Arlene: to the police, we'd all be strangers. They'd have nothing to go on. They'd have to start way back before the beginning—waste a lot of time—

RAY. I see Phyllis' point. She has a pretty fair knowledge of everyone in the house, and she knows detective methods. I think she's more competent to conduct an investigation than any outsider—any policeman.

LULU ANN. I do, too. I think Miss Deering is awfully clever, and I'm sure she could manage things right well.

PHYLLIS. Thank you, Lulu Ann.

MRS. MCCARTHY. *(Doubtfully)* But, Phyllis, the police might not like it—you're supposed to notify them immediately in a case like this.

PHYLLIS. Just give me a couple of hours, Mrs. McCarthy. If I haven't recovered your diamonds by then, you can call the police. It's a gamble, I admit—but I'm anxious to do this only for your sake.

ARLENE. That sounds fair enough, Hon.

SELENA. I think tho, too.

MRS. MCCARTHY. Do you really think you can get them back, Phyllis? Oh, dear—I wonder what the first Mr. McCarthy would want me to do.

RAY. It seems to me you've got everything to gain and nothing to lose, Mrs. McCarthy.

MRS. MCCARTHY. *(After a short pause)* Well, what is it you want me to do, Phyllis?

PHYLLIS. Tell me all the circumstances—anything you think would be helpful. I want you all to do that. First of all, Mrs. McCarthy, you'll have to tell me where those diamonds were kept.

MRS. MCCARTHY. *(Sighs; shakes her head; points to* LULU ANN*)* They were kept in her room.

LULU ANN. *(Starts)* In *my* room? (RAY *looks at* LULU ANN *anxiously; her hand involuntarily goes to her heart.)*

MRS. MCCARTHY. Yes. There's a little spring door under that picture of Mercury, dearie—that's where I kept them.

LULU ANN. *(A little too glibly)* To think of all

those diamonds being in my room all that time, and my never knowing.

MRS. MCCARTHY. It's a room I've never rented before, but when you came to the house, it was the last room we had vacant and, of course, I could just look at you and tell immediately that you were all right.

LULU ANN. Oh, thank you, ma'am.

PHYLLIS. Very well! The diamonds were in a wall safe in Lulu Ann's room. And I presume you had the only key to that safe, or is it a combination lock?

MRS. MCCARTHY. No, an ordinary lock, and I had the only key.

PHYLLIS. And that's why you wanted Lulu Ann in this room—so you could get your diamonds?

MRS. MCCARTHY. Yes.

SELENA. Thay, if they were in Lulu Ann'th room, couldn't thomeone have got in through the window and thtolen them?

LULU ANN. Oh, no, ma'am. I always keep my window locked, except when I'm sleeping.

PHYLLIS. All right. Now, what made you decide to get your diamonds this morning, Mrs. McCarthy?

MRS. MCCARTHY. (Sighs) I suppose you'll have to know sooner or later. I was going to sell them.

PHYLLIS. Sell them—after all these years?

MRS. MCCARTHY. Yes. The first Mr. McCarthy said to me before he passed on to his reward, "Now, Mazie, you put these diamonds away in a safe place, and some day you'll get your price for them."

PHYLLIS. I see. And you finally were getting your price.

MRS. MCCARTHY. (Nods) A man called me the other day—he was acting for a syndicate of European buyers.

PHYLLIS. Called you on the telephone? Do you mean to say you never saw this buyer?

MRS. McCARTHY. Of course I saw him—I'm not that dumb. We discussed the whole thing in his office.

PHYLLIS. And you were going to deliver the diamonds to him today—alone?

MRS. McCARTHY. Certainly not. They were sending a car for me—and an armed guard.

PHYLLIS. When?

MRS. McCARTHY. They were to be here at twelve-fifteen.

PHYLLIS. Who's got the time now?

SELENA. I have. *(Looks at wrist watch)* It'th twelve-twenty-five on my watch, but my watch ith ten minuteth thlow, tho it'th really twelve-thirty-five.

MRS. McCARTHY. Why, that's strange. They should have been here before this.

PHYLLIS. I'm afraid they'll never be here. And that buyer of yours, Mrs. McCarthy—I have a hunch you'll never see him again.

MRS. McCARTHY. But I don't understand. He had an office, and a letter of introduction to me from a gentleman in Europe—Amsterdam—

PHYLLIS. No doubt. But letters can be forged, and offices hired by anyone—even thieves. But we'll find out soon enough. Was there a telephone in the office?

MRS. McCARTHY. There was. I have the number right here. *(Opens purse and takes out an address book; leafs through it until she finds number)* Here it is: Mr. Pierre Remski. Hudson oh-six-oh-four-five.

PHYLLIS. Arlene, call that number, will you, and see if you can locate Mr. Remski.

ARLENE. All right, Hon! *(Takes address book, crosses to the telephone and dials a number.)*

LULU ANN. But, ma'am, why would they want to tell Mrs. McCarthy they were buying her diamonds if they weren't?

PHYLLIS. I can think of a very good reason.

ARLENE. *(In telephone)* I'm calling Hudson oh-six-oh-four-five— Yeah, that's right— What?—Are you sure?—You are?—Oh, all right—thanks, Hon. *(Hangs up)* The telephone's been disconnected.

ALL. *(Exclamations)* What! Disconnected! *(Etc.)*

PHYLLIS. That settles it. Your Mr. Remski was a confederate—a confederate of somebody in this house.

MRS. McCARTHY. But I don't understand—why—what—?

PHYLLIS. It's simple. They had to find out where you kept the diamonds, and they used this ruse to make you show them. When you went to the wall safe a little while ago to get the collection, was the safe locked, or was it open?

MRS. McCARTHY. No, it was locked.

PHYLLIS. Exactly! And the other day, when you first received the offer from Mr. Remski, I suppose you went to the safe to examine the collection?

MRS. McCARTHY. Why, yes, I did— I—it was only natural—

PHYLLIS. Of course—it was only natural. They counted on that. Someone was watching you in this house to find out where the safe was. After that, it was an easy matter to make a wax impression and get a duplicate key made.

MRS. McCARTHY. *(Looks at her; shakes her head uncomprehendingly)* But— Oh, I can't believe it! One of my own girls— It isn't pos— *(Suddenly)* That Miss Verne! That's her! The minute I laid eyes on her I knew—

PHYLLIS. Now, just a minute! We can't jump at conclusions, Mrs. McCarthy. The first thing we've got to do is—

CLAUDIA. *(Comes rushing in excitedly c. from L.)* Mrs. McCarthy! Mrs. McCarthy!

MRS. McCARTHY. Well, what is it? What's the matter with *you?*

CLAUDIA. I've been robbed.

ALL. *(Exclamations)* What! Robbed! Heavens! *(Etc.)*

PHYLLIS. You, too?

CLAUDIA. What do you mean—me, *too?*

PHYLLIS. Never mind. What's been taken?

CLAUDIA. My necklace. The most valuable possession I have in the world.

SELENA. Oh, that lovely pearl necklath, Claudia?

CLAUDIA. Yes. I could never replace it—it was a gift, presented to me by a very dear friend of mine —a very dear friend indeed. (PHYLLIS *shakes her head in dismay at this latest development, paces the room several times, thinking.)* Well, why doesn't somebody do something? Mrs. McCarthy, I'll hold you respon—

PHYLLIS. When did you have the necklace last?

CLAUDIA. Only last night. I wore it when I went out.

SELENA. Yeth, I remember theeing it then.

CLAUDIA. And I intended wearing it again today. I had a very particular appointment, doncha know. But when I looked for it in my jewel case, it was gone.

ARLENE. Well, looks like they didn't overlook a bet, doesn't it?

SELENA. I'd better check up on my five-and-ten thtuff.

CLAUDIA. What do you mean?

MRS. McCARTHY. They mean that while you've been worrying about your precious little trinket, somebody's made off with all my lovely diamonds— the McCarthy Collection.

CLAUDIA. They've been stolen too?

MRS. McCARTHY. Unless they walked out of here by themselves.

CLAUDIA. That settles it. There's a thief in this house— *(Crosses to arch.)*

PHYLLIS. Where are you going?

CLAUDIA. To report the matter to the police, of course.

PHYLLIS. Mrs. McCarthy has given me two hours to try to recover her diamonds. We've all agreed to leave the police out of it until those two hours are up.

CLAUDIA. Two hours? The pearls could be a hundred miles away by that time. If Mrs. McCarthy wants to waste her time with a lot of amateur detectives, that's her concern. But I don't, and I'm going—

ARLENE. Aw, why don't you be a sport, Hon? If you want to get your junk back—

CLAUDIA. *(Indignantly)* Junk?

ARLENE. Oops! Pardon me. If you want to get your valuable possessions back, Hon, your best bet is to give Phil a little co-operation. *(The OTHERS all nod ad lib. expressions of agreement.)*

CLAUDIA. Well— *(Hesitates)* Just two hours, then I go to the police. *(Comes back into room.)*

PHYLLIS. Thanks, Claudia.

CLAUDIA. But I certàinly do think every room in this house should be searched.

ALL. Yes. I do, too. That's a good idea. *(Etc.)*

PHYLLIS. It's probably just a waste of time, but if it will make you all feel better, let's have the search.

LULU ANN. Who's going to do the searching, ma'am?

PHYLLIS. Claudia, it was your idea. You can be the Sherlock Holmes.

CLAUDIA. Not I! I dislike snooping into other people's affairs, doncha know.

PHYLLIS. They're your pearls. You can identify them if they do turn up. And you'd better go along, Mrs. McCarthy.

MRS. McCARTHY. *(Rises)* All right!

SELENA. Can I go too, Phyllith? I've alwayth wanted to be a detective.

PHYLLIS. Yes, go ahead, Selena.

RAY. You can start with my room.

PHYLLIS. Oh—

RAY. Please. I insist on it. (PHYLLIS *shrugs.*) Come along. *(They cross to arch.)*

PHYLLIS. And let me know if you find anything that looks at all suspicious. (MRS. McCARTHY, CLAUDIA *and* SELENA *exeunt* C. *to* R.)

LULU ANN. I just can't imagine, ma'am, that anyone in the house would do such an awful thing as that. They all seem to be such fine people.

ARLENE. Yeah, all but the "duchess." She's a little too smooth for my taste.

LULU ANN. She seems awfully nice to me, ma'am. And besides, she wouldn't steal her own pearls, would she?

ARLENE. Maybe not, Hon. But as far as I'm concerned, she's public enemy number one in this house.

PHYLLIS. Until this thing is solved, Arlene, we're all under suspicion: you, I—all of us.

ARLENE. That's an idea. Maybe I walk in my sleep. You ought to look into it.

ROSIE. *(Enters* C. *from* L. *Stands in arch)* Vhere Mrs. McCarthy iss?

ARLENE. With the other bloodhounds on the trail, Hon.

ROSIE. Bloodhounds—? Ach, you're joost making foolishness. Lunch iss all ready vonce. Tell everybody und come downstairs. *(Turns to go.)*

PHYLLIS. Just a minute, Rosie.

ROSIE. Yah?

PHYLLIS. I need your help. You see, there's been a theft committed in the house—

ROSIE. *(Blankly)* T'st, t'st! Vhat's dot—"theft"?

PHYLLIS. Burglary! There's been a thief here.

Rosie. Ach, my goodness! Bandits in der house iss? T'st, t'st, you don't tell me! Could you beat it? Vhat's been shtolen already?

Phyllis. Miss Vandermeer lost a pearl necklace, and the McCarthy Collection is missing.

Rosie. McCarthy Col—Col—? Vhat's dot?

Phyllis. Never mind. But perhaps you can be of some help to us.

Rosie. Yah, sure—anything. I don't like those bandits—they're bad peoples, yah. Vhat I can do?

Phyllis. Try to answer a few questions intelligently.

Rosie. Yah, sure! Shoot!

Phyllis. Well, when you made up the rooms this morning, was there any bed that had not been slept in?

Rosie. My goodness, dot's a hard vone. Vait, I think— *(Wrinkles her brow in thought.)*

Phyllis. It's important. Try to remember.

Rosie. Yah, I try. *(Beams)* Yah, dot's right, sure. There vas vone.

Phyllis. Whose?

Rosie. It vas—it vas— *(Sighs in despair)* Golly! I don't remember her name.

Arlene. Describe her, Hon. What's she look like?

Rosie. Vell, she's got a long face—like a horse a liddle—und she's so high— *(Holds out her hand)* No, so high, maybe— *(Lifts it much higher.)*

Phyllis. Never mind her dimensions. What room is she in?

Rosie. Let me see—she's in one of the rooms, I know dot. Yah—top floor front, next to der "duchess."

Arlene. Miss Verne!

Rosie. Yah, sure—dot's right, Miss Verne. I knew it all der time, but it slipped off my tongue.

Phyllis. Thank you, Rosie—thank you very much.

ROSIE. Yah, yah. Iss dot all?

PHYLLIS. That's all for right now.

ROSIE. So, you come downstairs to lunch vonce. I got fried potatoes pancakes vith apple sauce, und you got to eat them vhen they're hot.

PHYLLIS. All right. We'll be down.

ROSIE. Sure. Und if there's anything else you vant to know vonce, you joost ask me. *(Exits c. to R.)*

LULU ANN. Why did you want to know that, ma'am—I mean about Miss Verne not sleeping in her bed last night?

PHYLLIS. Well, that little fact *may* mean, Lulu Ann, that she's far away from here by now, with the McCarthy Collection and Claudia's pearls.

ARLENE. Then the old gal was right about her after all.

PHYLLIS. *(Muses)* She might have been. She might have been.

ARLENE. Then, Hon, oughtn't we call the cops and get them on her trail right away?

PHYLLIS. I don't think so—not yet. I've got a hunch Miss Verne will be back before long.

ARLENE. What makes you think she will—if she's got the stuff?

PHYLLIS. Call it just a hunch. In the meantime, there are other things to be done. Besides Miss Verne, is everyone in the house now?

ARLENE. I guess so. All except Hannah and Grayce— *(Suddenly as she says "Grayce")* Grayce! And her concert!

PHYLLIS. Yes, I've thought about that.

ARLENE. That's where she got the five hundred. It must be—! Well, who would have thought Mrs. Pader-roos-ki would turn out to be a jewel thief—?

PHYLLIS. *(Smiles)* You're being just a little hasty, I'm afraid, Arlene.

ARLENE. But it fits, Hon—it fits perfectly. Up until today, Grayce didn't have the five hundred to give her concert, did she? All right. Today she has it, and she won't tell us where or how she got it. I can only see one answer to that.

PHYLLIS. I can see several answers to it. All we have in Grayce's case is a not-too-plausible motive. And I daresay each one of us in the house had that. Some of us could have used the money.

ARLENE. Yeah, no question about that.

PHYLLIS. And Lulu Ann, here—well, Lulu Ann loves diamonds.

LULU ANN. *(Starts)* Why—why—how did you know that, ma'am?

PHYLLIS. *(Smiles reassuringly)* You said so the other night.   *(WARN Curtain.)*

LULU ANN. *(Ill at ease)* Did I? Well, I—I do. I do love diamonds. I reckon nearly every girl does. But of course—

PHYLLIS. No, of course! You wouldn't steal them. But the point is we can find motives galore if we look closely enough. Our job is to find the right one—the motive that fits the crime. There's Hannah—

LULU ANN. Oh, ma'am! You don't think *she* took them?

PHYLLIS. No, I don't. That is, I don't know. But, psychologically, Hannah is the—the borrowing type.

ARLENE. I'll say she is.

PHYLLIS. She likes to acquire things. If the opportunity presented itself— *(Shrugs)* Who knows?

LULU ANN. But, ma'am, it couldn't have been Hannah. Why, she's a fine, sweet girl—

CLAUDIA. *(Enters C. from R.)* Oh, yeah? *Who's* a fine, sweet girl?

LULU ANN. Why—Hannah, ma'am.

CLAUDIA. She's a fine, sweet crook—that's what she is.

PHYLLIS. Why, Claudia, what do you mean?

CLAUDIA. I mean—this! *(Holds up a pearl necklace.)*

ALL. *(Exclamations)* The necklace! Your pearls! You found it! *(Etc.)*

PHYLLIS. Good work, Claudia! Where did you find it?

CLAUDIA. I didn't find it—Mrs. McCarthy did— under the pillow in Hannah's bed! *(The OTHERS exclaim in shocked surprise, as:)*

QUICK CURTAIN

ACT THREE

THE TIME: *Immediately following the Second Act. There is no elapsed time.*

THE PLACE: *The same.*

AT RISE: EVERYONE *is discovered just as at the end of Act Two.* PHYLLIS, CLAUDIA, ARLENE *and* LULU ANN *on stage. They are talking excitedly, ad-libbing among themselves.*

PHYLLIS. *(Trying to get their attention)* Just a minute! Please—just a minute! *(They quiet down)* You say you found your pearls in Hannah's bed, Claudia?

CLAUDIA. Yes.

PHYLLIS. I suppose there's no chance they might have come there accidentally?

CLAUDIA. Well, it seems to me that would have had to be a very unusual accident, doncha know.

PHYLLIS. You found your pearls, but the diamonds?

CLAUDIA. *(Shrugs carelessly)* Really, they're of no interest to me. I believe Mrs. McCarthy and those other persons are still searching, although it's quite obvious that Hannah either has them with her or she's disposed of them by now.

ARLENE. It certainly would seem so, Hon. I guess you had the right dope about Hannah.

PHYLLIS. It does look that way, doesn't it?

63

LULU ANN. I can't believe it of her—I just can't believe it. I'm sure she'll have some good explanation

CLAUDIA. *(Back to her customary bored manner)* She probably will, girlie—criminals always do. But that won't prevent me from preferring charges against her. *(Yawns sleepily)* It's been a trying day, hasn't it?

PHYLLIS. You'll still give me my two hours, won't you, Claudia?

CLAUDIA. Just as you wish. *(Yawns again)* Oh, dear! I believe I'll go back to bed. *(Crosses to arch)* I'll be in my room if you wish to see me, Phyllis.

PHYLLIS. All right!

CLAUDIA. And good luck, Miss Sherlock! *(Looks at PHYLLIS, laughs scornfully and exits C. to R.)*

ARLENE. That had all the earmarks of a dirty laugh, Hon.

PHYLLIS. Oh, well! *(Sighs)* It looks like our case is over—

ARLENE. Looks that way.

PHYLLIS. And yet—it doesn't quite jibe. There's something wrong with the picture.

ARLENE. What?

PHYLLIS. Well, if Hannah really is the criminal, why did she take the diamonds with her, but leave Claudia's pearls under her pillow?

ARLENE. With all those McCarthy rocks, Hon, why should she bother about baubles?

PHYLLIS. That's just the point—she wouldn't have bothered with it at all. And if she had, she certainly wouldn't have left them in the most obvious hiding place in h r room. *(Muses; shakes her head)* No, it just doesn't click, Arelne.

LULU ANN. Excuse me for buttin' in, ma'am; I don't know much about this detecting, but—mightn't the pearls and the diamonds have been taken by two different people?

PHYLLIS. No, I don't think— *(Thinks; snaps her fingers; excitedly)* Yes! Lulu Ann, I think you've hit on something—

LULU ANN. Oh, have I, ma'am?

PHYLLIS. That would explain a lot of things— things for which there isn't any explanation now.

ARLENE. Wouldn't that be quite a coincidence, Hon—two thieves stealing two things in the same place at the same time?

PHYLLIS. Perhaps it would, but coincidences sometimes do happen, you know. *(Crosses to arch)* I want to have a look at something. Come along, Arlene?

ARLENE. Sure. What have I got to lose? *(Crosses to her.)*

PHYLLIS. Want to come too, Lulu Ann?

LULU ANN. No, ma'am. I'll stay here. *(Laughs a forced laugh)* Two's company, you know, ma'am.

PHYLLIS. Just as you wish. *(As she and ARLENE exeunt C. to R.)* If this pans out, Arlene, it may be the end of— *(They are off.)*

LULU ANN. *(After they are gone, crosses up to arch, looks after them, then surreptitiously goes to telephone, dials a number, and after a moment begins to speak in a low voice)* Hello, Grand Central? I want to find out when's the next train to Alabama, Pikesboro— Well, I reckon Montgomery's the nearest stop to it— I said Mont— *(Hangs up quickly as she sees RAY coming into the arch C. from R.)*

RAY. Calling someone?

LULU ANN. *(Nervously)* Er—yes, I had to make a call, ma'am—on business.

RAY. I see. *(They come down into room.)*

LULU ANN. I—I don't believe that about Hannah, do you, ma'am?

RAY. It looks very bad for her—they found the pearls right in her bed.

LULU ANN. But she isn't a criminal— I'd almost swear to that, ma'am.

RAY. Why? What makes you so sure?

LULU ANN. I don't know, I'm just sure. I reckon I never saw a criminal that I knew about, but Hannah just doesn't *look* like one to me.

RAY. They never do. *(At divan)* Come here and sit down with me, my dear.

LULU ANN. Well, I—I haven't time—

RAY. Please! I want to talk to you.

LULU ANN. *(Hesitates)* Well—all right. *(They sit on divan together.)*

RAY. I want you to tell me something of yourself. You don't mind, do you?

LULU ANN. Oh, no, ma'am—I don't mind.

RAY. Have you been happy, my dear?

LULU ANN. *(Puzzled at this attitude)* Happy? Well, yes, ma'am. I reckon I've been just a sort of carefree kid. *(Laughs)* That's what folks say back home.

RAY. And your grandfather—that nice old grandfather you spoke about—he has been kind to you?

LULU ANN. Oh, yes, indeed, ma'am. He's really the nicest old gentleman you'd ever care to meet. He couldn't have treated me any better if he'd been my own father.

RAY. I'm glad to hear that, my dear. *(Looks at her with infinite tenderness)* I don't suppose you remember your own parents, your father and your—your mother.

LULU ANN. No, ma'am, I can't say I do. And Grandpop never seems to talk much about them, either. But I'm sure they must have been very fine people.

RAY. Oh, yes. I—I'm sure of that, too.

LULU ANN. Once I did see a picture of my mother—

RAY. *(Startled)* You did?

LULU ANN. Uh-huh! It was in an old box up in our attic. I was just a kid at the time. When Grandpop discovered me up there going through the box he was very angry, and he took it away and never let me see it again. I could never quite understand why he did that, ma'am, but he always refused to even talk to me about it after that, so I sort of forgot it in time. It came back to me just now while we were talking.

RAY. I see. Well, I'm sure he must have had some very good reason for doing what he did.

LULU ANN. Yes, ma'am. I reckon he did. *(Pauses; looks at her)* Why—why are you talking to me like this, Miss Cartwright?

RAY. Oh—I'm just interested.

LULU ANN. Well, I didn't think you were, after what you said a little while ago.

RAY. I know, my dear. It may be hard to believe— but perhaps I had my reason.

LULU ANN. I'm sure you must have, ma'am.

RAY. *(Looks at her keenly)* Someone in this house has been doing some very kind things for me, so Mrs. McCarthy tells me. That someone isn't by any chance you?

LULU ANN. Me? Why, I—I don't know what you mean, Miss Cartwright.

RAY. No? Well, never mind. But it was very sweet of you just the same, Lulu Ann, and I—well, I guess there just isn't anything for me to say.

LULU ANN. *(Looks at her and smiles)* No, ma'am —reckon there isn't.

RAY. But that isn't exactly what I wanted to speak to you about, my dear. You know this—this is a very serious business, about Mrs. McCarthy's diamonds—

LULU ANN. *(Looks away, frightened)* It certainly is.

RAY. And anyone involved in it—no matter how

innocently—may find herself in a very difficult situation.

Lulu Ann. I know that, ma'am, but—but what of it? What are you telling this to me for?

Ray. *(Takes her hand)* Because, my dear, if there's something you know about it—*(Tenderly)* I believe the wisest thing you could do would be to tell Miss Deering now.

Lulu Ann. What makes you think I know anything?

Ray. I can't tell you how I know that. I just do.

Lulu Ann. Well, you're wrong, ma'am—you're wrong.

Ray. Please, my dear, you can trust me.

Lulu Ann. *(Pulls her hand away from her)* I tell you I don't know anything about Mrs. McCarthy's diamonds—not a thing. *(Rises and crosses to window)* I—I don't know what gave you such an idea, ma'am.

Ray. *(Rises; crosses to her)* Please listen to me, Lulu Ann. I don't want to see you getting into trouble, and you're going to, if you don't—

Rosie. *(Enters c. from l.)* For the second time I'm telling you lunch is— *(Breaks off and looks around)* My goodness! Vhere is everybody vonce?

Ray. Why—they're around, I imagine, Rosie.

Rosie. Do they vant to starve to death already? They're usually in such a hurry for der food, und today it's on der table half an hour yet, und nobody comes.

Ray. We're all upset because of Mrs. McCarthy's great loss.

Rosie. Ach, yah! Dot's terrible, ain't it?

Ray. It certainly is.

Rosie. T'st, t'st! Shtill, you've got to eat, ain't it? Und my beautiful potatoe pancakes, they're getting spoiled up. Please, did they find the bandits yet?

Ray. Not yet, but I'm sure they will.

Rosie. Yah! Vell, if nobody else vants my pancakes, looks like I got to eat them myself. *(Turns to go)* Maybe you vould like a nice cup of coffee?

Ray. Not I, thank you— *(TELEPHONE rings.)*

Rosie. Oh, vould you answer it, please? Sometimes I don't understand the peoples so vell. I guess they joost don't talk plain enough.

Ray. Surely. *(Crosses to telephone and answers it)* Hello— Yes— Who? Miss Day?—Yes, she's in. Hold on, please. *(Puts receiver down)* It's for Miss Day.

Rosie. Yah, I call her vonce. *(Takes a step off R. and calls)* Miss Day! Der telephone!

Arlene. *(From off R.)* Okay, I'm coming!

Rosie. So. If you vant lunch, you better make up your mind in a hurry, because potatoe pancakes is my favorite vegetable. *(Exits C. to L.)*

Arlene. *(Entering C. from R.)* Did she say telephone?

Ray. Yes, for you, Arlene.

Arlene. Thanks, Hon. *(Picks up receiver)* Hello-oh!—Oh, Looie— *(Disgustedly)* Yeah— Yeah— What? *Me?*—Well, I should say not!—No, never in a million years— Selena?—Not her, either— Well, I'll ask her, if it'll make you feel any better, but I know what her answer will be— Yeah, I can't talk now, Looie; I'm standing up to my ears in jewel thieves— Oh, nothing; I'll tell you some other time. G'bye. *(Hangs up)* Of all the crack-brained ideas! Guess what he wants now, Hon.

Ray. I haven't the slightest idea.

Arlene. He and the boy friend want to enter a dance marathon, and they want Selena and me to be their partners. Can you beat it—a *dance marathon!*

Ray. Selena would just love that, wouldn't she?

Arlene. Yeah. Her and her feet. That Looie can

think of more ways of making a woman suffer than anyone I know.

RAY. Has Phyllis discovered anything new?

ARLENE. I don't know—she's still looking. I did find a silk scarf in Hannah's room that I had forgotten I owned. She must have borrowed that scarf two months ago, Hon, and this is the first I've seen of it since.

RAY. I suppose there's nothing that can be done now until Hannah returns.

ARLENE. I don't know. Phil thinks now she didn't have anything to do with it.

RAY. Oh, she—she must have. If not Hannah, who else?

ARLENE. *(Shrugs)* Search me, Hon. Phil's theories have got my head in a whirl—I mean, even a worse whirl than usual.

RAY. I do hope everything will be cleared up soon.

ARLENE. Yeah. *(To* LULU ANN*)* What's the matter with you, Hon?

LULU ANN. *(Who has been lost in her thoughts, starts)* Matter—? Oh—oh, nothing, ma'am. Why?

ARLENE. You look as if you'd just lost your best friend. Cheer up, Kid—they can't give you more than twenty years for lifting a few diamonds.

LULU ANN. What! I— *(Angrily)* How dare you say that? I'll have you know I—

RAY. *(Anxiously)* Lulu Ann!

LULU ANN. The very idea of intimating that I stole those diamonds! I won't stand—!

ARLENE. Wait a minute, Hon—hold your horses. Can't you take a little joke?

LULU ANN. *(Dazed)* Joke—? Well, I— Oh! *(Runs and throws herself into divan.)*

RAY. *(Follows her over and sits with her)* There's nothing to be alarmed about, my dear. Arlene was only joking, don't you see? *(*ARLENE *looks at them curiously, wondering what it's all about.)*

PHYLLIS. *(Enters* C. *from* R. *She's carrying a bulky envelope and a sheet of note paper)* I think we're finally getting some— *(Breaks off as she notices* LULU ANN*)* Why, what's the matter with Lulu Ann?

RAY. It's nothing at all, Phyllis. She had a little nervous spell, but she's all right now.

PHYLLIS. Well, no wonder, after what's happened in this house today.

RAY. Yes.

PHYLLIS. Don't you want to go up to your room and lie down for a while, Lulu Ann?

LULU ANN. *(Sitting up)* Thank you, ma'am. I feel all right now.

RAY. She'll be quite all right, Phyllis.

ARLENE. Have you got some more clues there, Hon?

PHYLLIS. I certainly have. Listen to this: *(Reads from paper)* "As soon as you've located the stuff, try to contact X and let me know what you can find out about her. I know she's in the house, and she's clever. Don't take any chances and watch your step with her. If you need help let me know." And it's signed "Chief."

ARLENE. What's it mean, Hon?

PHYLLIS. "As soon as you've located the stuff"— don't you see, that *might* mean the diamonds.

ARLENE. Yeah, and then again it might not. It may be just a harmless note, Hon.

PHYLLIS. If it's just a harmless note, why the absence of names, and the use of "X" and "Chief"?

RAY. I think Phyllis is right, Arlene. It certainly sounds mysterious enough.

ARLENE. You haven't told us where you found it yet.

PHYLLIS. I know. If it does mean anything—and I have a hunch it does—it rather balls up my other theory. Because I found it in Miss Verne's room.

RAY. Miss Verne! Dear me, do you believe it's she after all, Phyllis? Then what about Hannah?

ARLENE. Yeah, and what about a lot of other things? *(Shakes her head as if to clear it)* Whew! What a merry-go-round!

PHYLLIS. I'd give a great deal to know who "X" is. She's in the house, and she's clever, and you can't take any chances with her.

ARLENE. *(Suddenly)* I've got it.

PHYLLIS. You have?

ARLENE. Sure, Hon! Lulu Ann was right, don't you see—?

LULU ANN. Me?

ARLENE. Yeah, when you said there were two crooks. "X" is Hannah, and she certainly was clever —didn't she fool all of us? This Verne dame beat her to the rocks, so she had to be satisfied with the pearls—

PHYLLIS. Then why did she hide them under her pillow?

ARLENE. Well, you see— Huh? *(Pauses and scratches her head)* Gosh, I'll have to figure that out.

PHYLLIS. It's a very pretty theory, except for that one little weak point.

ARLENE. Yeah. Weak points seem .to be what we've got nothing else but around here.

PHYLLIS. What's the time now, Lulu Ann?

LULU ANN. *(Looks at her watch)* It's just about two-fifteen, ma'am.

PHYLLIS. Those two hours are nearly up. I'll have to get busy.

ARLENE. You certainly will, Hon, at the rate we've been going up to now.

PHYLLIS. Well, there's still— *(Holds up the envelope)* This.

ARLENE. What is it?

PHYLLIS. *(Sighs)* Just another clue. And I haven't even got a theory about this one—

GRAYCE. *(Enters* C. *from* L.*)* Good afternoon, everyone. *(They ad lib. "Hellos.")* Well, I've taken the fatal step!

PHYLLIS. Fatal step?

GRAYCE. My concert—it's all arranged.

PHYLLIS. *(Without enthusiasm)* How nice!

GRAYCE. It's to be the week of— *(Notices the* OTHERS *staring at her)* Why, what's the matter? What are you all looking so glum about? *(They don't answer.)* Can't any of you talk? Nothing happened while I was gone?

ARLENE. Oh, no, Hon—not much!

GRAYCE. What do you mean?

PHYLLIS. The McCarthy Collection has been stolen, Grayce.

GRAYCE. The McCarthy Collection? The fabulous diamonds nobody ever saw? (PHYLLIS *nods.)* Good Heavens! A robbery! Well, have they caught the thief—who took them?

PHYLLIS. That's just what I'm trying to find out.

GRAYCE. You, Phyllis?

ARLENE. She's turned gumshoe on us, Hon. Mrs. McCarthy gave her two hours before she called the coppers, and the two hours are practically up.

GRAYCE. But—surely it isn't possible—you don't think that someone in the house took the diamonds?

PHYLLIS. That's exactly what I do think. It's impossible for an outsider to have got them.

GRAYCE. *(Aghast)* Good heavens!

ARLENE. We've been up to our ears in theories for the last hour, Hon, and it looks like anyone of us could have done it. So if you've got a confession to make, now's the time to spill it.

GRAYCE. *Me?* Don't be absurd.

PHYLLIS. I would like to ask you a few questions, Grayce.

GRAYCE. Certainly. Anything I can do to help—

(Notices the envelope in PHYLLIS' *hand)* Why—why—what are you doing with that?

PHYLLIS. I'm sorry. I found this in your room—

GRAYCE. *(Indignantly)* Found it? You mean you *took* it out of the drawer of my dresser. *(Snatches the envelope out of her hand.)*

PHYLLIS. But, Grayce—

GRAYCE. The idea! What right have you got to go prying into my personal affairs? *(Looks into the envelope, satisfying herself the contents have not been disturbed.)*

PHYLLIS. We all agreed it was necessary to search *everyone's* room.

GRAYCE. *(Very angry)* Well, I didn't agree. Nobody asked me about it. You aren't a police officer, you haven't a warrant—and you had no right in there.

PHYLLIS. I'm sorry you feel that way about it, Grayce—

GRAYCE. Well, this is a fine time to be sorry.

PHYLLIS. But the fact remains that there is one thousand dollars in bills in that envelope— *(Exclamations of surprise from the* OTHERS.*)* And I'm afraid you'll have to explain how you got it.

GRAYCE. *(The* OTHERS *stare at her expectantly as she pauses before replying)* So! You think *I* took the diamonds. Is that it?

PHYLLIS. *(Patiently)* Someone in this house took them, Grayce. No one is free from suspicion. All I ask you to do is clear yourself—if you can.

GRAYCE. *If* I can? There won't be the slightest difficulty about that.

PHYLLIS. I'm glad, then, for your sake.

GRAYCE. My father was a poor man—he'd worked hard all his life, for forty years, and all he'd been able to save in that time was one thousand dollars—in a government Liberty Bond. Before he died, ten years ago, he gave me the bond and made me prom-

ise I'd never sell it, except in a moment of direst
need. It was his idea that if anything ever happened
to me, if I got sick—that bond would see me
through. Well, you all know how I've been saving
for my concert—

ARLENE. Yeah.

GRAYCE. I was tired of waiting, discouraged. I
knew if I was ever going to get anywhere with my
music, it would have to be soon. So, much as I hated
to do it, I sold my father's bond.

PHYLLIS. *(After a pause)* I see. I'm sorry, Grayce
—but naturally—well, we had to make sure.

GRAYCE. Perhaps this will help to convince you—
(Opens her purse, and gives her a paper) Here.

PHYLLIS. *(Takes it; looks at it)* Bill of sale made
out to Grayce Johnston for one United States
Liberty Bond, series of nineteen-eighteen. Sold for
one thousand dollars and dated yesterday. *(Hands
it back to her)* Forgive me, Grayce. *(There is an
awkward little pause.)*

RAY. I'm sure she understands, Phyllis.

GRAYCE. I'm not so sure I do. You might have had
a little confidence in me. After all, we've known
each other a long time.

PHYLLIS. I never really doubted you, Grayce.

GRAYCE. You had an odd way of showing that.
And now, if you're entirely finished with me—if
you're *quite* sure you don't want to turn me over to
the police— *(Crosses to arch)* Excuse me! *(Exits
angrily C. to R.)*

PHYLLIS. I should have stuck to "Grandma's
Recipes."

RAY. She'll get over it, Phyllis. Naturally, she was
disturbed.

PHYLLIS. *(Sighs)* A detective's life is a hard one.

ARLENE. Anyway, we've eliminated one suspect,
Hon. That narrows it all the way down to about
thirty-seven.

LULU ANN. *(Rises)* Will you excuse me, ma'am?

PHYLLIS. Certainly, Lulu Ann.

LULU ANN. I think I'll go to my room and get a little rest. *(Crosses to arch.)*

PHYLLIS. Yes, surely. Do that.

MRS. MCCARTHY. *(Entering* C *from* R. *with* SELENA*)* Where do you think you're going, dearie?

LULU ANN. Why—just up to my room, ma'am.

MRS. MCCARTHY. You'd better wait. You'll be interested in what I've got to show you.

PHYLLIS. Did. you find something, Mrs. McCarthy?

MRS. MCCARTHY. We certainly did.

PHYLLIS. Not the diamonds?

MRS. MCCARTHY. No, not the diamonds. I've been over every square inch of this place with a fine-comb, and I didn't find them—but I expect to.

ARLENE. What makes you think you will, Hon?

MRS. MCCARTHY. *(Grimly)* This! *(Holds up a small key.)*

PHYLLIS. The key to the wall safe?

MRS. MCCARTHY. *One* of the keys to the wall safe, Phyllis. Because there's two of them. *(Takes another key from her pocket)* This one is mine. You can see for yourself—they're as alike as two peas in a pod. *(The* OTHERS, *except* LULU ANN, *crowd around her, looking at the keys.)*

LULU ANN. *(Looking very frightened)* I think I'll— I don't feel so—

MRS. MCCARTHY. No, you don't feel well, do you, dearie? And it's my guess you'll feel a lot worse when you get through explaining how this key came to be in your room.

ALL. Lulu Ann! (RAY *drops downstage; sits in chair down* R., *her eyes staring out over the audience.)*

LULU ANN. I—I don't know anything about it.

MRS. MCCARTHY. Oh, yes, you do.

LULU ANN. If you found that key in my room, ma'am—somebody must have dropped it there.

MRS. McCARTHY. Yes, I suppose they dropped it in the drawer of your dresser, and I suppose it got up and wrapped itself in your handkerchief without any help from you.

PHYLLIS. Is that where you found it?

MRS. McCARTHY. It certainly is.

SELENA. That'th right.

PHYLLIS. I'm afraid you'll have to explain, Lulu Ann.

LULU ANN. *(Wildly)* Explain? There's nothing to explain—! You can't do anything to me—you can't! I haven't done anything wrong—!

MRS. McCARTHY. I want my diamonds.

LULU ANN. I haven't got them. I don't know anything about—

MRS. McCARTHY. *(Doggedly)* You give me my diamonds, or I'll call the police.

PHYLLIS. Please, Mrs. McCarthy—this isn't getting us anywhere. Perhaps I can—

MRS. McCARTHY. She had the key—that's proof enough for me. She knows where those diamonds are, and I want them.

LULU ANN. *(On the verge of hysteria)* Why do you keep *saying* that—? I tell you I don't know—I don't know anything about the diamonds, ma'am, I d-d-don't!

PHYLLIS. Really,, Mrs. McCarthy, the girl's becoming hysterical—

MRS. McCARTHY. Why wouldn't she be? She's just a little thief, that's what she—

LULU ANN. Oh, please, ma'am, won't you believe me? What would G-G-Grandpop say if he knew I was in all this trouble? Ooohhh—! *(As she starts to cry she pulls out a handkerchief from her sleeve, and a small object falls to the floor.)*

MRS. McCARTHY. What's that! *(They ALL stare*

as she stoops and picks it up) It's one of them—one
of the McCarthy Collection! *(The* OTHERS *look at*
LULU ANN, *waiting for an explanation.)*

LULU ANN. *(Stares at the diamond, her eyes
opened wide in wonder)* Why—why—where did
that come from?

ARLENE. Looks to me like it came from the sleeve
of your dress, Hon.

PHYLLIS. Where did you get it, Lulu Ann?

LULU ANN. Why, I—I don't know, ma'am. It
must've fallen out of my sleeve, but I—I just can't
imagine how it got there.

MRS. McCARTHY. Well, I can. Phyllis, call the
police.

LULU ANN. You're not going to have me arrested,
ma'am?

MRS. McCARTHY. I certainly am. We've wasted
enough time. And to think I let you take me in like
you did.

LULU ANN. But I didn't, ma'am— I tell you I
didn't. *(Pleading)* Don't call the police, please,
ma'am—not yet. Give me a chance—

MRS. McCARTHY. All right, I'll give you a chance.
Will you hand over the rest of my diamonds?

LULU ANN. I can't. I can't. I haven't got them.

MRS. McCARTHY. Phyllis, if you won't call the
police, I will— *(Starts for arch.)*

RAY. Wait.

MRS. McCARTHY. You better keep out of this,
Ray.

RAY. I'm afraid it's too late for that. *(Rises)* You
see, I'm in it already—very much in it.

PHYLLIS. Ray! What do you know about it?

RAY. Everything! Lulu Ann is quite right, Mrs.
McCarthy. She didn't take your diamonds—

MRS. McCARTHY. If she didn't, who did?

RAY. *(Quietly)* I did. *(She is standing down* C.,
the OTHERS *all staring at her. They don't see* MISS

VERNE, *who enters* C. *from* R. *and stands taking it all in.)*

LULU ANN. *You,* ma'am? You took the diamonds?

RAY. I did.

PHYLLIS. I'm sorry, but I can't believe that.

RAY. Whether you believe it or not, Phyllis, **it's true.** And I'm ready to take my punishment.

MRS. McCARTHY. Where are they? Where are my diamonds?

RAY. Oh—er—where are they *now,* you mean?

MRS. McCARTHY. Yes.

RAY. Why, I—I haven't got them. I disposed of them.

MRS. McCARTHY. *(Excitedly)* Disposed of them? Disposed of the McCarthy Collection? Where did you dispose of them?

RAY. I'm sorry, I'm not at liberty to say. However, you can call the police. I'm quite ready.

PHYLLIS. Just a minute, Mrs. McCarthy. Ray, I don't know what your purpose is in confessing to a crime you didn't commit, but I'm morally certain you didn't take those diamonds.

RAY. Really, don't be absurd, Phyllis. Why should I say I had if I hadn't?

PHYLLIS. I'm not sure, but I think I can make a pretty good guess. Shall I try?

RAY. *(Quickly)* No. I—I took them. The diamond I—I planted in Lulu Ann's sleeve is proof enough of that.

MRS. McCARTHY. This is too much for me. I'm going to call the cops and let them figure the whole thing out.

MISS VERNE. Lose some diamonds, Mrs. McCarthy? *(They ALL whirl to face her.)*

MRS. McCARTHY. You—? What do you know about it?

MISS VERNE. That depends. *(In businesslike*

manner) Is everyone in the house now—all the girls?

RAY. Really, Miss Verne, there's no need to concern yourself in this. I've told Mrs. McCarthy—

MISS VERNE. Yeah, I heard what you told her. That sort of melodramatic scene might go on the stage, but it's no good here.

RAY. *(Nonplussed)* Why—why—!

MISS VERNE. Will someone kindly tell me if all the girls are in the house?

ARLENE. Sure, Hon—all but Hannah.

MISS VERNE. Hannah? Who's that? Oh, the Williams girl! All the others here?

PHYLLIS. I think, before we answer any more of your questions, it might be a good idea for you to answer one or two of them yourself.

MISS VERNE. *(Impatiently)* Please, Miss Deering, I'll thank you not to interfere.

PHYLLIS. *(Indignantly)* Interfere? Well, suppose you tell us just who you are and what you're doing here.

MISS VERNE. Later. Just now I—

PHYLLIS. And then there's the little matter of a certain note we'd like to have you explain—remember? A note signed, "Chief."

MISS VERNE. Note—? See here, have you—?

CLAUDIA. *(Enters C. from R. in street clothes)* Well, your two hours are about up, aren't they, Phyllis? *(Smiles scornfully.)*

PHYLLIS. Yes, but—

MISS VERNE. How do you do, Miss Vandermeer?

CLAUDIA. H'lo!

MISS VERNE. Going out?

CLAUDIA. Yes, a little airing, doncha know.

MISS VERNE. Oh, sure. Mrs. McCarthy tells me she's missing a few diamonds.

CLAUDIA. Yes.

Miss Verne. So I think it might be a good idea if we searched you, Miss *Vandermeer*.

Claudia. *(Momentarily drops her pose of boredom)* Why, you—you! Search me—? I'll show— *(Recovers herself)* You're being quite too absurd, doncha know.

Miss Verne. Am I?

Claudia. In the first place, who are you?

Miss Verne. In the first place, and every other place, I'm Helen Verne, and I'm employed by the Grand Mutual Assurance Society, insurers of the McCarthy Collection. (Others *exclaim in surprise.*) If there's any doubt— *(Takes out a business card and hands it to* Claudia.*)* Perhaps this will convince you.

Claudia. *(Looks at card)* Well, what if you are? Surely you don't suspect me? Why, I—I was robbed myself—

Miss Verne. Really?

Claudia. Of these pearls. You should know how valuable they are. Luckily they were recovered.

Miss Verne. *(Unconvinced)* How fortunate for you.

Claudia. Yes, wasn't it?

Miss Verne. Then, if you're innocent, you can't have any objections to a little search.

Claudia. Why, I—I— *(Thinking rapidly)* No—no, of course not.

Miss Verne. Good. *(Steps over to her and expertly runs her hands up and down her person)* I'll take that, please. *(Indicating* Claudia's *purse.)*

Claudia. *(Shrugs)* You're the doctor. *(Hands it over.* Miss Verne *opens it and looks through it. Shakes her head in disappointment. Hands it back.)* Are you quite satisfied?

Miss Verne. No, not quite. Take your shoes off.

Claudia. What! Look here, this is going too far.

Miss Verne. Take them off. (Claudia *stares*

angrily at her for a moment, then sits in divan and takes them off. MISS VERNE *taps first one heel, then the other)* Ah! I thought so! *(Pulls one of the heels off and from the inside of it pours a number of diamonds onto table* C.*)* And there's your McCarthy Collection!

MRS. McCARTHY. *(Overjoyed)* My diamonds! Glory be! My diamonds! *(Gathers them up.)*

MISS VERNE. Are they all there?

MRS. McCARTHY. I think so—let me see. *(Counts them)* Yes, with the one I got before, they're all here—every blessed one of them!

MISS VERNE. In the future, take my advice and keep them in a bank vault. Save yourself a lot of grief.

MRS. McCARTHY. I will. I certainly will. As the first Mr. McCarthy used to say—

MISS VERNE. Sorry, haven't the time. Here's your shoes, Lil. Put them on and let's get going. *(Tosses the shoes to her.)*

PHYLLIS. Lil?

MISS VERNE. *(Smiles)* Lil Cooper, society crook. Wanted in a number of cities—yes, *quite* a number, hey, Lil?

CLAUDIA. I'm not talking until I see a lawyer.

MISS VERNE. *(Shrugs)* Suit yourself. But step on it and let's get going.

MRS. McCARTHY. I don't know how I can ever thank you, Miss Verne. I knew from the minute I laid eyes on you that you was a person I could have a lot of confidence in, and the first Mr. McCarthy always thought I was the most marvelous judge of human—

MISS VERNE. That's all right—you don't have to thank me. It's all in the day's work to me.

MRS. McCARTHY. Be that as it may, you'll find me a very grateful woman. I'm going to see that you're properly rewarded.

Miss Verne. Well, thank you very much.

Mrs. McCarthy. Yes, indeed. I'll speak to your employers first thing in the morning and ask them to give you a raise of salary.

Claudia. *(Rises)* Oh, cut the gab and let's be on our way.

Miss Verne. Right. Are you going to be a nice little girl, Lil, or do I have to get out the bracelets?

Claudia. Bracelets is one kind of jewelry I never wear, girlie.

Miss Verne. Okay! *(Crosses to arch with her)* Oh, I'll send for my bag in the morning, Mrs. McCarthy. I'm afraid you're going to have a room to let.

Claudia. Two rooms. Come on, sleuth.

Miss Verne. See you later, folks. *(They exeunt c. to L.)*

Phyllis. Boy! No more Philo Vance-ing for me. Whoever said "Shoemaker, stick to your last," certainly uttered a mouthful.

Selena. Maybe I'm awfully thtupid, but there'th thtill a lot of thingth I don't underthtand. Who put the pearlth in Hannah'th bed and the diamonth on Lulu Ann?

Phyllis. There's nothing very mysterious about that—now. It was all done by Claudia, or Lil, or whatever you want to call her.

Arlene. But why, Hon?

Phyllis. Her first and only thought, probably, was to get out of here without being searched. So, from her viewpoint, anything she could do to becloud the issue was that much gravy.

Mrs. McCarthy. Ray, what was the idea in saying you took them?

Ray. I—I don't know.

Mrs. McCarthy. You don't know? Well, that's a nice one—you might have been in jail this minute.

LULU ANN. I reckon I know. You did it to shield me, didn't you, ma'am?

RAY. *(Confused)* No, no! I—well, you see— Perhaps some other time, please—we've all had enough of this for a while.

PHYLLIS. But how did you ever get the key, Lulu Ann? That's what *I* don't understand.

LULU ANN. I found it on top of my dresser last night, ma'am. Then I was trying to rearrange the furniture in my room, and I discovered the little safe under the picture. I tried the key and it worked, so I opened the safe, but there was nothing in it. Then, when I found out that's where Mrs. McCarthy had kept her diamonds, I was afraid you-all would think I had taken them.

PHYLLIS. You should have told us. It would have been much simpler.

LULU ANN. Yes, ma'am. Reckon it would, but—

ROSIE. *(Enters c. from L.)* Miss Day, there's a chentleman downstairs to see you vonce. He say his name iss "Looie."

ARLENE. That's nice, Hon. Tell him I'll be back a week from Saint Patrick's Day.

ROSIE. *(Puzzled)* You mean you don't vant to see him?

ARLENE. You get the idea.

ROSIE. T'st, t'st! Dot's too bad. *(Turns to go)* Und he has such a nice motor machine—

SELENA. An automobile! Arlene, did you hear the thame thing I did?

ROSIE. But vait vonce—

ARLENE. Halelujah! No more sore feet! Come on, Hon! *(They rush out c. to L. at top speed.)*

ROSIE. Vait, vait—! Ach, I vas going to tell them it ain't no automobile—it's a bicycle.

MRS. MCCARTHY. Rosie, have you started on dinner yet?

ROSIE. Not yet. I don't know vhy, but my stomach

don't feel so vell. Maybe it's der potatoe pancakes, hah? Shtill, I only had fourteen of them, und dot's not many.

MRS. McCARTHY. What were you planning to have?

ROSIE. I thought maybe hamburger vonce?

MRS. McCARTHY. No, that won't do. Tonight we must have something special— I feel like celebrating. Let's see, let's see— I have it! We'll have mushroom sauce on the hamburger.

ROSIE. Yah, dot's nice.

MRS. McCARTHY. Well, go on, get started, get started. I'll go with you and help you myself. This has got to be good. Come on, come on. *(Bustles off c. to L., followed by ROSIE.)*

RAY. Well, it's all over, isn't it?

PHYLLIS. Apparently.

LULU ANN. Pardon me, ma'am, but I don't believe it's quite all over yet.

RAY. Why, how do you mean?

LULU ANN. I mean I haven't thanked you yet for trying to take the blame of something you thought I did. I—I didn't know you were such a real friend of mine, ma'am.

RAY. It was nothing, my dear.

LULU ANN. Why did you do it?

RAY. I'd rather not discuss it, do you mind?

PHYLLIS. I believe she has a right to know, Ray. *(Pointedly)* That, and several other things.

RAY. *(Flustered)* Why—why—

(WARN Curtain.)

PHYLLIS. In my search of the rooms, Ray, naturally I couldn't overlook yours. Quite inadvertantly, I came across a number of documents. They were very interesting—and I'm quite sure they'd prove more so to Lulu Ann.

RAY. *(Alarmed)* Please, Phyllis—! You can't— you don't know what you're doing!

PHYLLIS. I think I do. I admire the spirit of self-sacrifice. It's a favorite theme of all authors. But I believe it can be carried too far—

RAY. In the name of Heaven, Phyllis—you mustn't—!

PHYLLIS. I think I must. I think every girl has the right to the love of her own mother. And I think mothers have a certain duty to their daughters.

LULU ANN. What! What are you saying, ma'am?

PHYLLIS. Well, it seems a long time ago an actress named Ray Cartwright had a little girl whom she called Lulu Ann—

LULU ANN. My heavens! *You*, ma'am? (RAY *stands there, her head bowed.*) But why—how—? I don't understand—

RAY. *(After a pause)* It's a long story and— Oh, don't be too angry with me, my dear—

LULU ANN. *Angry*—? Oh, ma'am! (RAY *clasps her in her arms and holds her hungrily.* PHYLLIS *stands watching them and smiling to herself.*)

HANNAH. *(Bursts in* C. *from* L.*)* Oh, Kids— I have the most *marvelous* news!

PHYLLIS. Really?

HANNAH. The most romantic thing that ever happened to me. Guess what!

PHYLLIS. I can't.

HANNAH. So romantic! Just like a love story in a magazine! I never was so thrilled—you're looking at the future Mrs. Sylvester Crookingham!

QUICK CURTAIN

DANGER—GIRLS WORKING!

PROPERTY PLOT

Furniture:
>Divan.
>Grand piano.
>Piano bench.
>Long table.
>Round table.
>Console table.
>Three armchairs.
>Floor lamp.
>Table lamp.
>Rug.

On Stage:
>Drapes, curtains, on window.
>Pictures, on wall.
>Books, ashtrays, etc.
>Telephone, on console table.
>Cushions on chair down L.
>Sunday paper (Act II).

Off Stage:
>Telephone bell.
>Doorbell.

Hand Properties:
>Act I.
>>Newspaper (ARLENE).
>>Tablecloth (ROSIE).
>>Three books (PHYLLIS).
>>Linen (ROSIE).
>>Suitcase (LULU ANN).
>>Paper money (LULU ANN).
>>Handkerchief (RAY).

Act II.
   Book (PHYLLIS).
   Lace scarf (ROSIE).
   Clip (MRS. McCARTHY).
   White gloves (HANNAH).
   Watch (SELENA).
   Address book (MRS. McCARTHY).
   Pearl necklace (CLAUDIA).
Act III.
   Bulky envelope (PHYLLIS).
   Note paper (PHYLLIS).
   Paper (GRAYCE).
   Two small keys (MRS. McCARTHY).
   Handkerchief (LULU ANN).
   Small piece of glass (LULU ANN).
   Business card (MISS VERNE).
   Shoe with false heel (CLAUDIA).
   Small pieces of glass (CLAUDIA).

DANGER—GIRLS WORKING!
PUBLICITY THROUGH YOUR LOCAL PAPERS

The press can be an immense help in giving publicity to your productions. In this belief we submit a number of suggested press notes which may be used either as they stand or changed to suit your own ideas and submitted to the local press.

The ——— Players of this city have secured the rights to present for the first time in this community the successful new three-act comedy, "Danger—Girls Working," by James Reach. This play, in the short time it has been available for production, has secured for itself an enviable reputation among audiences wherever it has been shown.

"Danger—Girls Working," according to ——— ———, who is in charge of the production for the ——— Players, presents an absorbing and realistic picture of a group of girls trying to get along in the big city by their labor, wit and resourcefulness. Never before, says Mr. ———, has there been a play which dealt so competently and so sympathetically with this phase of urban life. He is confident that this distinguished comedy will prove to be one of the most successful stage plays ever shown in this locality.

Tickets for "Danger—Girls Working" may be procured at ———. It will be played beginning ——— for ——— nights only at ———.

****

With ——— ——— heading the cast of ten, the ——— Players are now in the midst of rehearsals for their forth-coming production, "Danger—Girls Working," a new comedy in three acts by James Reach.

89

Also featured prominently in the cast are ————
————, ———— ————, ———— ————, ————
————, and ————. The entire production is under
the personal supervision of ———— ————, who
describes "Danger—Girls Working" as one of the
best plays of its type he has ever encountered in the
theater. The story, briefly, is about a group of girls
living together in the big city and trying to make
their way despite the handicaps and hardships that
beset them. Mr. ———— is confident that this brilliant
new comedy will establish itself as one of the best
ever to be shown here.

"Danger—Girls Working" will be shown for ————
nights only beginning ———— at ————. Tickets are
now on sale at ————.

****

James Reach, author of "Danger—Girls Working," the new three-act comedy which will be the
next presentation of the ———— Players of this community, has, during a long and varied career in the
theater, written some twenty plays. These plays, too
many to be enumerated here, have become famous
throughout the country. There is not a single state
in the Union, and in fact not many towns and vil-
lages of any size, that have not at some time or
other witnessed at least one of the many hits from
the pen of this popular writer.

"Danger—Girls Working" bids fair to equal or
exceed in popularity anything that Mr. Reach has
written heretofore. In the short time since its
national release, it has won the unqualified plaudits
of audiences wherever it has been shown, and ————
————, who is directing the forthcoming production
for the ———— Players, is confident that it will set
a new high-water mark in local stage history.

Tickets for "Danger—Girls Working" may be
procured at ———— for the performance which will
take place on ———— at ————.

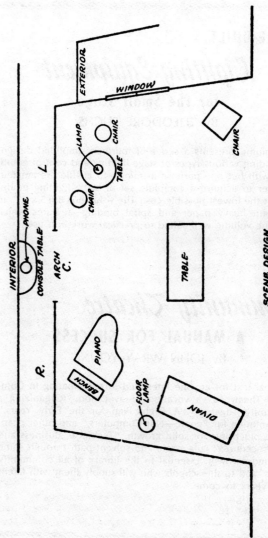

SCENE DESIGN
"DANGER – GIRLS WORKING!"

HOME-BUILT

Lighting Equipment

for The Small Stage

By THEODORE FUCHS

This volume presents a series of fourteen simplified designs for building various types of stage lighting and control equipment, with but one purpose in mind—to enable the amateur producer to acquire a complete set of stage lighting equipment at the lowest possible cost. The volume is 8½" x 11" in size, with heavy paper and spiral binding—features which make the volume well suited to practical workshop use.

Community Theatre

A MANUAL FOR SUCCESS

By JOHN WRAY YOUNG

The ideal text for anyone interested in participating in Community Theatre as a vocation or avocation. "Organizing a Community Theatre," "A Flight Plan for the Early Years," "Programming for People—Not Computers," and other chapters are blueprints for solid growth. "Technical, Business and Legal Procedures" cuts a safe and solvent path through some tricky undergrowth. Essential to the library of all community theatres, and to the schools who will supply them with talent in the years to come.

HANDBOOK

for

THEATRICAL APPRENTICES
By Dorothy Lee Tompkins

Here is a common sense book on theatre, fittingly subtitled, "A Practical Guide in All Phases of Theatre." Miss Tompkins has wisely left art to the artists and written a book which deals only with the practical side of the theatre. All the jobs of the theatre are categorized, from the star to the person who sells soft drinks at intermission. Each job is defined, and its basic responsibilities given in detail. An invaluable manual for every theatre group in explaining to novices the duties of apprenticeship, and in reassessing its own organizational structure and functions.

"If you are an apprentice or are just aspiring in any capacity, then you'll want to read and own Dorothy Lee Tompkins' A HANDBOOK FOR THEATRICAL APPRENTICES. It should be required reading for any drama student anywhere and is a natural for the amateur in any phase of the theatre."—George Freedley, Morning Telegraph.

"It would be helpful if the HANDBOOK FOR THEATRICAL APPRENTICES were in school or theatrical library to be used during each production as a guide to all participants."—Florence E. Hill, Dramatics Magazine.

BUSY SPEAKER'S
POCKET PRACTICE BOOK
(Revised and enlarged)

By Belle Cumming Kennedy and Patricia Challgren. A foreword by Wilton L. Haverson, M.D., Dr. P.H. Diagrams and illustrations by Robert W. Teeter. A concise manual of tested exercises for voice and speech improvement prepared for public speakers, actors, clergymen, students and teachers. Written for those who are prepared to give a few minutes every day to the building of music, power and clarity into speech. It provides material for at least the first year of voice and speech practice. This is not a text book. It is a practice book, made to fit your hand, to lie flat on the desk, to stand upon a shelf. Spiral binding.

PRACTICAL AID FOR THE
INEXPERIENCED SPEAKER

By Belle Cumming Kennedy. A handy, quick-reference aid for anyone who wants to present his best personal appearance as a speaker before any type of audience. There are many methods and techniques presented in these twelve short lessons, all designed to give to the inexperienced speaker an understanding of the art of holding an audience. Among the lessons are: Developing Your Confidence; Planning Your Speech; Style; Platform Delivery; Introducing Speakers; and Points of Etiquette. A companion manual to The Busy Speaker's Pocket Practice Book. Spiral binding.

HERE'S HOW

A Basic Stagecraft Book

**THOROUGHLY REVISED
AND ENLARGED**

by HERBERT V. HAKE

COVERING 59 topics on the essentials of stagecraft (13 of them brand new). *Here's How* meets a very real need in the educational theater. It gives to directors and others concerned with the technical aspects of play production a complete and graphic explanation of ways of handling fundamental stagecraft problems.

The book is exceptional on several counts. It not only treats every topic thoroughly, but does so in an easy-to-read style every layman can understand. Most important, it is prepared in such a way that for every topic there is a facing page of illustrations (original drawings and photographs)—thus giving the reader a complete graphic presentation of the topic along with the textual description of the topic.

Because of the large type, the large size of the pages (9″ x 12″), and the flexible metal binding, *Here's How* will lie flat when opened and can be laid on a workbench for a director to read while in a *standing* position.

Other Publications for Your Interest

AGNES OF GOD
(LITTLE THEATRE—DRAMA)

By JOHN PIELMEIER

3 women—1 set (bare stage)

Doctor Martha Livingstone, a court-appointed psychiatrist, is asked to determine the sanity of a young nun accused of murdering her own baby. Mother Miriam Ruth, the nun's superior, seems bent on protecting Sister Agnes from the doctor, and Livingstone's suspicions are immediately aroused. In searching for solutions to various mysteries (who killed the baby? Who fathered the child?) Livingstone forces all three women, herself included, to face some harsh realities in their own lives, and to re-examine the meaning of faith and the commitment of love. "Riveting, powerful, electrifying new drama . . . three of the most magnificent performances you will see this year on any stage anywhere . . . the dialogue crackles."—Rex Reed, N.Y. Daily News. ". . . outstanding play . . . deals intelligently with questions of religion and psychology."—Mel Gussow, N.Y. Times. ". . . unquestionably blindingly theatrical . . . cleverly executed blood and guts evening in the theatre . . . three sensationally powered performances calculated to wring your withers."—Clive Barnes, N.Y. Post.   (#236)

**(For Future Release.
Royalty, $60–$40, when available.)
(Posters available)**

COME BACK TO THE 5 & DIME, JIMMY DEAN, JIMMY DEAN
(ADVANCED GROUPS—DRAMA)

By ED GRACZYK

1 man, 8 women—Interior

In a small-town dime store in West Texas, the Disciples of James Dean gather for their twentieth reunion. Now a gaggle of middle-aged women, the Disciples were teenagers when Dean filmed "Giant" two decades ago in nearby Marfa. One of them, an extra in the film, has a child whom she says was conceived by Dean on the "Giant" set; the child is the Jimmy Dean of the title. The ladies' reminiscences mingle with flash-backs to their youth; then the arrival of a stunning and momentarily unrecognized woman sets off a series of confrontations that upset their self-deceptions and expose their well-hidden disappointments. "Full of homespun humor . . . surefire comic gems."—N.Y. Post. "Captures convincingly the atmosphere of the 1950s."—Women's Wear Daily.   (#5147)

(Royalty, $60–$40.)